HEALING, ROMANCE & REVOLUTION

LETTERS FROM A YOUNG AMERICAN NURSE IN 1926 CHINA

COMPILED BY

CAROLYN *and* DENNIS BUCKMASTER

BOOK PUBLISHERS NETWORK

Book Publishers Network
P.O. Box 2256
Bothell • WA • 98041
PH • 425-483-3040
www.bookpublishersnetwork.com

10 9 8 7 6 5 4 3 2 1

Printed in the United States of America

LCCN 2011945644
ISBN 9781937454203

Editor: Barbara Kindness
Cover Designer: Laura Zugzda
Typographer: Stephanie Martindale

Several of the expressions, terms, and spellings herein, while not in current usage, were left as Harriet wrote them in her letters so the reader can enjoy her true, authentic correspondence.

Contents

Who's Who

Name	Role/Relationship
Archer, Mr. aka Paddy	Irishman Hat met on *SS President Jefferson*
Beeby, Nell	Staff nurse
Blacks, The	New to Changsha and looking to be involved with Hunan Bible Institute
Branch, Dr.	Hospital Superintendent after Dr. Yen resigned
Brundage, Helen	Superintendent of Nurses whom Harriet replaced in 1926
Burke Gordon	American Consul, Nanking
Burke, Gordon	Standard Oil manager
Chang, Harry	Hospital Staff Dentist
Chao Hu Tai	Governor of Hunan Province
Chiang Kai-shek	Leader of the Nationalist Party, the Kuomintang (KMT), from 1925 until his death in 1975; a close ally of Sun Yat-sen
Ching, Dr. Sarah	In charge of Obstetrics
Farnam, Dr. Louise	One of first women admitted to the Yale School of Medicine. Graduated first in her class. Taught and practiced medicine for ten years in China. Great friend and mentor to Harriet

Name	Role/Relationship
Feely, Mr	Representative of local steamship company
Gage, Miss Nina	Registered nurse in China from 1908 to 1927. Later was in charge of the nursing program at Hsiang-Ya Hospital and is widely credited for pioneering modern nursing in China. Head of Hospital and School; also, President of the International Council of Nurses.
Gilberts, The	Family from Yakima
Gladys Trivetta Box	Nurse
Greene MD, Phil	Hospital doctor
Greene, Ruth	Wife of Dr. Phillip Greene. Harriet lived for a time in the Greene home.
Gregory, Ralph	Standard Oil manager
Guominjun, The	Military faction very sympathetic to Sun Yat-sen's Kuomintang regime in Guangzhou . Due to geographic isolation, they were independent of one another.
Hail, Reverend WJ	Professor of History and Board Member
Hartman, Dr. and Mrs.	Doctor associated with the hospital
Harveys, The	Managers of the C and A Mission Home
Hasenpflug, Miss	Apparently a faculty member.
Heinrichson, Mr and Mrs.	Friends of Harriet. Occupation unknown.
Henry, Elizabeth "Hank"	Longtime friend.
Hertig, Mrs.	Shipboard acquaintance
Hewitt, "Sandy"	A gentleman friend who had strong romantic interest in Harriet
Hirota, Miss	Japanese acquaintance
Houston, Dr.	Staff doctor
Howard, Mrs.	Shipboard acquaintance on her way to Manila, The Philippines.
Hutchins, Frank	Charlie Keller's roommate
Hykes, The	Standard Oil executive
Jen, Dr.	A graduate of the local Medical School

Name	Role/Relationship
Keller, Charlie	Staff member and future fiancé of Harriet. Charlie was born and raised in China of Britishers who later lived in Cleveland, Ohio.
Kiaer, Mr.	Executive with the YMCA
Lenzel, Southard	Eligible bachelor
Lewis, Clarice	Secretary to Dr. Yen
Li, Dr. and Mrs. S.Y.	Friends of Harriet and a favorite staff doctor and his wife.
MacGregor, Mr.	Skipper of an Alaska vessel
Mariano, Mr	Captain of Italian gunboat
McKillop, Marjorie	Girl from Seattle who lived in Northern China
Monroe, Dr.	Professor from Columbia on the *SS President Jefferson* and on his way to Peking
Moore, Mr.	Asiatic Petroleum Manager held for ransom
Norelius, Jessie	Also known as "Jess." Registered nurse who served in China from 1924 through 1938. Becoming dean of the school of nursing at Hsiang-Ya School of Nursing
Osawa, Mr and Mrs	Friends in Kyoto
Ouwerkirk, Mr.	Worked for Asiatic Petroleum Company and had rowing shell
Plumer, Mrs.	Acquaintance on board the *SS President Jefferson*
Pye, Watts O.	Shanxi, China-based Congregational missionary. Well-known and liked; died in 1926 at age forty-eight
Smith, Austin	Hat's brother
Smith, Dr. Clarence	Hat's father, a prominent physician in Seattle
Smith, Eunice	Hat's sister, married to Harry Smith
Smith, Harold	Hat's cousin who had been in Changsha for several years, even before she first went to China in 1921. Taught Geology and was Interim Treasurer of Yali in early 1920's
Smith, Harry Edwin	Eunice Smith's husband. Economic Professor, University of Washington
Spurling, Miss	In charge of Missionary Home

Name	Role/Relationship
Strong, Sidney Reverend	Congregationalist minister from Seattle, WA; was a pacifist and practitioner of the social gospel and active with the Industrial Workers of the World (I.W.W.). Had a strong impact on Harriet in her more radical years
Tang, Dr.	Involved in T.B. research
Tsao, Mr	Hospital Manager
Tyng, Wally	Head of the Episcopal Mission
Valpy, Mr	Manager or executive of the railroad
Vincent, John Carter	Apparently a staff member, and bit of ladies' man who stole Charlie Keller's wife.
Vincent, Margaret	Fetching sister of John Carter Vincent
Walker, Charles Lester (Les)	Teacher at Yali Middle School, companion, friend, and later Hat's romantic interest. Became a writer for *Harper's* and *The New Yorker* magazines
Walters, Dr. Ota	Staff doctor in charge of X-Ray and peer of Dr. Louise Farnam
Wooten, Mr.	Executive/Manager with A.O. Steamship Line
Wu Pei Fu	Major figure in the struggles between the warlords who dominated Republican China from 1916 to 1927.
Yamasaki, Mr.	Acquaintance in Yokohama
Ye Ting,	Kuomintang General
Yen, Dr. W.W. and Hilda	Hospital Superintendent
Zhao Heng Ti	One-time governor of Hunan Province
Zink, Miss	Previously doing TB work in Colorado; (1926) in Presbyterian Mission in Changteh

ACKNOWLEDGMENTS

Harriet Holbrook Smith for capturing her experiences and thoughts for generations to come. What a treasure!

Also, to Harriet Smith for bothering to capture well-composed photographs (with who knows what camera technology) significantly enriching our understanding of her experience and the book.

Russ McComb[1] (and family) and Doug McComb[2], who stored Harriet's boxes of "gold" without throwing them out as the boxes took up valuable storage and collected dust.

Thank you, Barbara Kindness, for recognizing the potential of Harriet Holbrook Smith's letters home. We suspected value; Barbara confirmed the value. Also, thanks for her expert editing. Ultimately, Barbara has provided invaluable help in making the necessary contacts in getting our book reviewed by influential players in the industry.

A call-out to Sheryn Hara and her expertise in drawing together a team of professionals in expediently bringing our project to fruition. Also thanks to Sheryn and Barbara in helping us settle on a title. Sheryn was exceptionally patient in helping us keep our bearings through the publishing process.

---

1. Carolyn's brother.

2. Carolyn's brother.

A huge round of applause for Carolyn's job of scanning more than 400 of Harriet's photographs, many of which are included in the book. Also, the dozens of hours spent matching text from the scanning to the word-processed document.

Thanks to Carolyn for closing the door to my office as I fought the computer, scanner and technology in transferring the text into word-processing software. I "mutter" a lot!

Thanks to myself for finding the process for capturing Aunt Hat's writing so others can enjoy her wit and wisdom. And, doing so without neighbors calling the police.

Thanks to all our friends, relatives and our coffee klatch group at Trilogy,[3] who patiently shared (mostly enthusiastically) our excitement in getting this labor of love out to the public.

Dennis

---

3. 55-plus community east of Redmond, WA

PROLOGUE

Harriet Holbrook Smith (1897-1989) lived a fabulous life of adventure, high educational achievement, world travel, professional accomplishment, wide friendships, and much more. "Hat," as she was fondly known, was an exceptional person, loved and respected by many. Her long career reached its pinnacle at the University of Washington where she retired as the Dean of the School of Nursing.

Seminal to her achievements were two "tours of duty" with the Yale-in-China[4] Program in Changsha, Hunan Province, China (1921-1924 and 1926-1927). These five years were filled with change in China—culturally, politically, socially, militarily, and so much more. Hat was right in the middle of these dynamic changes, discovering and developing her self-knowledge and world view; her understanding of humanity and human behavior, while

Harriet's Nursing Graduation

4. The Yale-China Association first incorporated as the Yale Foreign Missionary Society, and known informally as Yale-in-China as early as 1913. Originally, nondenominational, by the 1920's it ceased to be overtly missionary and was re-incorporated in 1934 as a secular organization, the Yale-in-China Association. In 1975 it became the Yale-China Association.

HARRIET SMITH

Harriet's tall handsome figure is quite in keeping with her deep manly voice and 'hail-fellow-well-met' manner. We fear that her ideas are rather anarchistic. Mount Holyoke is not accustomed to have its quiet green marred by the red flag of the I. W. W.'s while a ranting demagogue endeavors to rouse its peaceful inhabitants into rebellion thru stirring and gory speeches.

Harriet's Early Radical Roots

mastering management, leadership and diplomatic skills, and enhancing her wisdom.

Harriet matured from a "wild-eyed" political radical (see yearbook entry above), into a mature professional, manager and leader of men and women.

We could go on and on. Personally, I consider Hat as being the wisest person I have ever known.

The following letters home provide a "keyhole" vision into her last year in Changsha. Especially interesting is the evolution of political/revolutionary events from mostly an annoyance to tragedy and the eventual Hospital and School closure, which were reopened later and are still operating in China today.

You will discover how Hat mixes everyday experience, social engagements, entrepreneurship and war, love and romance, friendship and professional responsibilities, with balance, optimism, faith, hope and good humor.

Harriet At 90 Years Old

Please enjoy,

Carolyn and Dennis Buckmaster (Carolyn is one of Harriet's nieces)

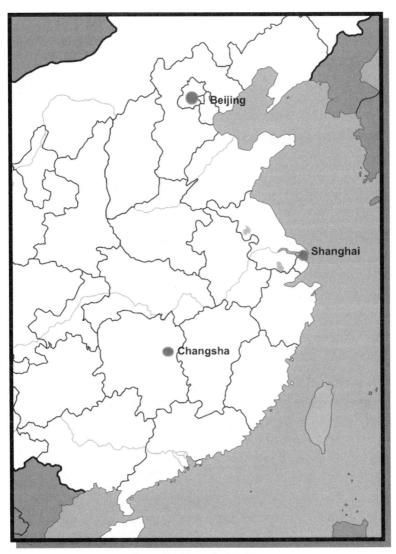

Changsha:Shanghai:Beijing

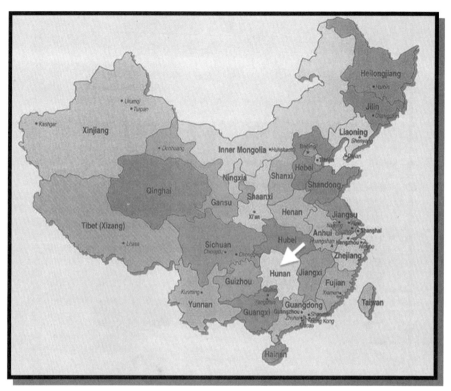

Originating from Haiyang Mountain in Lingui of Guangxi, the Xiang is the largest river in Hunan and one of the largest tributaries of Yangtze River. It is 856-km long and 670-km of it is in Hunan.

Harriet's Dilemma

Harriet spent almost four years in China (1921-1924), returning to Seattle in 1924 to work with her father, Dr. Clarence Smith, in his medical practice. By March of 1925 she was already wrestling with issues regarding returning to China and other personal and professional concerns. The following are excerpts of her letter to Miss Nina Gage, Dean of the School of Nursing, providing insight into Harriet's motivations and personal values.

March 10, 1925

Dear Miss Gage,

I hope you are duly impressed with the heading up top, which indicates my Dad and I have the electrocuting parlors going now. I wear a uniform and cap and all sorts of things, just like a nurse 'n everything. I am hoping it will give the establishment lots of face, although my honorable parent is rather fed up with expression, which I use to him when he wants to saw and hammer, or mend the electric light wires, or unscrew the plumbing. He remarks, "It seems you have learned a lot of foolishness in China." He is doubtless right, and I might add he does not know the half of it, and that it is not all the sort of foolishness that he thinks.

Thank you very much for the letter I received a couple of days ago. It finds me in somewhat of a quandary. I think I might quite truthfully say, were it not for family complications, I would agree to return to China in the fall. I cannot say I am much thrilled by the race and tear of business competition, which, though glorifying work, as the minister said last Sunday, still does not thrill one with its motive, however necessary. I remember one time, in the course of my wayward thoughts, I "thunk" to myself it would be good sport to stay a couple of years in China; and then a couple in the Philippines, and then a couple in India, etc., but somehow I reckoned, without the possibility I might by chance become attached to one of these places, which is just what has happened as regards China in general and Changsha in particular. I try to ponder carefully whether it is the idea of China or whether it is the idea of the H.Y.H. (Hsiang-Ya Hospital) that gives me a funny feeling, and as my time was nearly wholly spent in the latter institution, I naturally conclude it is the answer.

Hsiang-Ya Hospital

Now about things here, and how the wind blows, etc. For the present, I might modestly remark I am quite indispensable to my Father. He's not as young as he once was, but has the idea shared by many past middle life he is just as young as he ever was, and all that. I wouldn't go so far as to argue the subject, but I am quite willing to admit I think he is kidding himself. In other words, he's a bit old, though far from aged, but he does occasionally forget details, and sometimes doesn't quite grasp the situation quick as three winks, and trying out this new branch of electrotherapy he is absolutely dependent on me. Furthermore, the new equipment was a bit "costive" as Branch used to say, so the thought of hiring and training is a terrible thought in light of the other expenses. Of course, this is one of the things which we expect will be lightened after a few months, the expectation being we shall be so busy as to be obliged to work another assistant into the ropes. In that case, she would doubtless be quite capable of doing the mechanical part all right.

At present there is a very important aspect of morale which the daughter of the firm can impart, and which an outsider might not give. Therefore, the merest insinuation I might be thinking of fleeing to the ends of the earth instills great sorrow into the mind of both Father and Mother. Although they have brought us up under the teachings that missionaries are sort of saints on earth, and the most wonderful thing a person could be is a missionary, still they seem to have a rather different feeling when the matter is definitely applied to their daughter, yours truly. It seems odd, yet is one of the inconsistencies of which we are all guilty. They realize I can hardly expect to spend my declining years running a diathermy machine, or turning an ultraviolet light onto a skinny baby, but the idea of going back to China in the near future is a very distressing one. And, after all, in spite of my globetrotting tendencies, I appreciate the fact that I owe something to the peace of mind of my parents, however dull and uninteresting I may occasionally find the daily routine, and the rather stupid evenings.

I continue to nourish the sense of humor, which Aggie found so boorish and common, so I cannot say I am fading away under the present regime. I guess, therefore, the conclusion to all this harangue would be that, though I should like very much to definitely say I should like to be presented for reappointment—if that's the correct terminology—I cannot commit myself at this time. It is altogether possible affairs may be so arranged later on that I might be able to go, but am not sure now.

I sometimes wonder if the next Chinese New Year's might not be a good time to hike out. That's about the time of year someone usually is sick or gets engaged or something. Isn't that about right? I suppose the Board ought to go ahead and appoint the full quota of others, as I am so indefinite. All this indefinite business is very irksome; as I realize there is a danger in never accomplishing what one postpones too long. I shall avoid that pitfall. If you have any brilliant inspirations about the situation, I should be glad to hear them, but I cannot see anything to be done right now.

I'm getting to be a reg'lar Public Speaker. I usually hold forth twice a week or so, sometimes at luncheons, or at afternoon club meetings, and once at a tea where they took in $60. Shades of Strunky! All I need is 300 rice bowls and a Pennsylvania Dutch ancestry, neither of which I have. I get quite a kick out of it, which shows to what a depth I have fallen, and I sometimes think with horror of what my facetious little friends from China would say, if they were to see me!

Please remember me to any of the friends you may see in New York or New Haven or wherever, and with very best wishes to yourself,

Hat

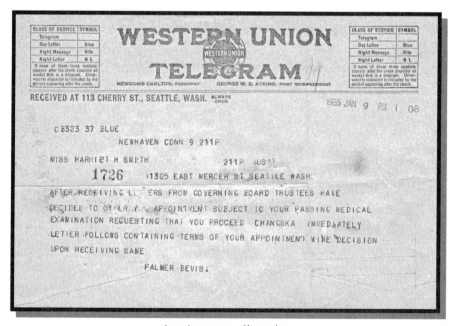

Appointment to Changsha

FEBRUARY 1926 TO FEBRUARY 1927

February 3, 1926 ~ Aboard *SS President Jefferson*

Dear Mother,

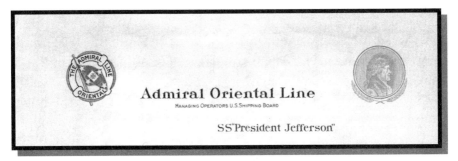

Just so you may have a word from the missing link for next week's session, I'll pen a note to go from Victoria (British Columbia, Canada). It was only a few hours ago I left my native shore but I've defied the elements by shoving down a large lunch, including Camembert cheese, which you must admit is brave or reckless. I had several candy boxes stowed and can't decide whether to eat 'em now while all is serene or wait until dinner each day or what. I may still have some to feed the friends at Changsha. I tell you it will be many a day before I forget the sight of you and the dear church beau hanging over the rail together waving a fond farewell. Do you suppose there's an omen in that—a sign that might link you together? Yes, I agree. Heaven forbid is right. You're correct.

You're correct. Stick to the banker!

Mrs. Fisher and son Peter are chaperoning a girl to Victoria. She's Julia's friend and will meet her fiancé returning on the Grant to be married at the Fishers'. That makes me think. How about the "D.H." beau meeting us as we return in 1927 just before the wedding in Seattle?

Enough—enough! I'm sitting at the First Officer's table. He is Mrs. Marion's brother-in-law, whose brother, Ted Marion, married the G. E. M. Pratt's daughter, and is a dentist. I haven't seen him yet as he is busy getting us underway.

The other person is a middle-aged woman with gray hair (horrors!) who lives in Alaska and knew this officer when he was a skipper on boats to Alaska. His name is McGregor in case our Alaska tourist friends travelled on his boat. Ask Mrs. Perk. This woman is a funny old girl with false teeth she cleans by the inhaling-plus-tongue method after meals. Very entertaining. She's going to make the round trip to Manila just for the ride. I can imagine more pleasant seasons in which to take a pleasure trip.

I'm so darned sleepy I think I'll hibernate for about a week and work up good steam for Japan and China. I've always thought these females who appear on the sixth or seventh day are interesting at least.

Admiral Oriental Line Stateroom

I think when I take the huge sleep I'll get the cabin boy to chauffeur in the Victrola and have Rose Marie and "Brown Eyes" to send me off. Not bad. There's a cabin a few doors from mine from whence issue sounds of heavy and serious imbibing so I suspect some little friend may not appear for a few days. It's great to be a mish. Bless your old hearts. Don't forget the "black tea with lemon."

February 4, 1926 ~ Aboard *SS President Jefferson*

Dear Mother,

I am enclosing a passengers' list. It looks as though we would be sufficiently exclusive. I never heard of any of them before except the Iverson name, Mr. and Mrs., came back with me before. He is a Philippine embroideries importer and lives in Manila. I suspect she may be the short fat Jewess who stood next to me as we sailed. With that size and shape only the Mr. called her "Momma." I'll write from day to day and send the result from Japan. I shall not go into details about the ship as you've seen it and the passengers are not so numerous. It looks like a quiet outfit.

Did you see the packet Dr. Strong gave me? All bound round with a big cord? It contains many numbers of the Christian Century, some copies of the YMCA magazine Tracy writes for, a Russian propaganda pamphlet, a couple of international journals, and a pamphlet of his on *The World's Best Man* "–a story of Jesus," and Anna Louise's *Children of Revolution*. It's an interesting collection to say the least. Jerry sent lovely daffodils, Aunt Cora, Katherine and Mr. Baldwin, candy, Mrs. E.L., a book of Carolyn Wells and poems, a book on the Bible. and a lovely perfume bottle. It's great to have one's friends take such an interest in a departure. After I started off I wondered to myself just what in blazes I left for. I'd really sort of become used to the home routine again. It will make it easier to come back next time, and that will be very soon really. I'm trusting Eunice to do the daughter act for me too for a while. With Dwight and Jo coming out this summer you'll have a finger on some of the children. I hope you will not find my junk too messy to throw away or stow away. I put some choice articles in the lower part of the chest. It's a good anti-moth place if you want to use it and don't mind the delicious smell.

I will really be more thoughtful in the matter of writing. Being used to the excitement of the Orient, I need not let it distract me this time. I'd like to be home again soon.

Ever so much love to you and Dad

I told Frank to take good care of you and he said he would!

SS President Jefferson

February 5, 1926 ~ Aboard *SS President Jefferson*

Dear Mother,

All's well so far, with me, at least, though I cannot say the same for all the other little friends. There are so few people around it's impossible to have anything in the sports line and then, it's much too rough.

We did not leave Victoria until midnight as there was a very strong wind blowing. That gave us a chance to be settled in bed when we finally got under way. All the things in my stateroom did the "Charleston," including flower vases, and finally the racks under my bed, used as sides during rough weather, went over with a crash. Everything squeaked and moaned and I had to have the porthole closed. Altogether it was not a huge success from the point of view of sleep. In the morning I made the fatal error of taking a bath. The bathroom was very hot and stuffy and when I came out I was damper than when in the water. I hastened to clothe myself though feeling very queer, and tottered out on deck. I had forgotten to set back my watch so was half an hour early for breakfast, if you can imagine it, so thought I'd start with a couple of "chuckanuts." I munched them cautiously, and after a few moments lost the dear things—too bad. I unanimously voted against further breakfast and snoozed most of the morning. I saw one or two men around but that was all. Since then I have consumed each meal with enthusiasm and have met Mr. McGregor at whose table I sit. The Alaska woman who should be my vis-à-vis, I have not seen since we left Victoria.

I had a lengthy session with the Dr. yesterday, conversational, not professional, and he is an interesting individual, writes stories but has never had one published, so you see what a bond there is between us. Then last evening I paced the deck with a very pleasant young Englishman going out in the Customs Service. He's an Oxford man and has taught at the University of California as well as traveling in Venezuela and other places. His father met up from Mexico to see him in New York. on his way across the country. He's very interesting, quotes Milton and Egyptian dynasties and all that, and by the way says someone has begun to decipher the Hittite language in which they describe the Trojan War.

Tell Arch an account appears in some Hellenic magazine.

A few feeble ones have come to life today and right now I have my eye on Dr. Monroe who is a Professor from Columbia on his way to Peking[5].

He had something to do with the expedition of Mary Duggan's Dad, went on to the Orient, and I met him in Kyoto in 1924. I think the Mrs. is with him though I haven't seen her.

Just spoke to the Second Officer named Egbert who used to live on Fifteenth Avenue and played with Almon Bogardus.

The weather has been fine except for rough water, sun all day today and a following wind. The sea gulls followed us until today. They are such graceful birds and sailed through the wind with so little effort.

I read "Wild Geese." I quite liked it. Though a bit gloomy and morbid it's good to have the old man get his, rather than have it all come out wrong.

The essays by Edward Newton that Eunice gave me are quite interesting. Many essays came out in the *Atlantic* Magazine, I think. I've also read some of the Carolyn Wells Anthology, which is amusing.

February 9, 1926 ~ Aboard *SS President Jefferson*

Dear Mother,

All the passengers are up these days, but even so we are rare, not like my trip home when the Chinese students were all over the place.

I sleep in a cabin across the hall with Mrs. Howard. She is a very sweet girl from Washington, D.C., who is en route to Manila to join

5. Now known as Beijing

her husband who is a Naval officer. She is very attractive, but not the very frivolous type and was so lonesome all by herself we combined forces. We talked after going to bed and it seems to cheer her nicely. She told me one very shocking fact: my friend Mary Aplin Barton, whose spouse is in Standard Oil in China, died this last fall following an operation for appendicitis. I don't know any details as she heard it through Mary's aunt in Washington. Isn't that sad?

There is another very gracious woman, the mother of a man in the Customs who is going to visit her son for three months. Her name is Plumer and she comes from Boston. She is quite typically Boston and very pleasant.

The young Oxford man is an Irishman after all. I have great fun with him, starting with a water fight two days ago, which ended in an exchange with the rope rings they use for quoits[6]. Then we threw the rings back and forth in a friendly but vigorous way yesterday, which was good exercise but strenuous. I still have a couple bruises from it. It's well to have someone so active around as it keeps me stepping and with so few people we do not have so many sports as usual. This noon we went up on top and were nearly blown overboard by the gale that was mostly wind and much hail and snow; losing his hat, but *this* Hat stayed put. Altogether, it's been fine weather, bright and clear, but a little rough, no real blizzard or anything like it.

Sunday, Mr. McGregor took Mrs. Howard, Mrs. Hunt—the Alaska woman—and me all over the ship. We saw the cold storage places and the kitchens, or galleys I should say, and the steerage and whatnot. It is hard to realize what a complicated organization it is without going over the whole place. Mr. McGregor is a fine chap and I enjoy being at his table.

February 15, 1926 ~ Aboard SS *President Jefferson*

Dear Mother,

I see I did not mention the 155 dead Chinese aboard, being taken home for burial; also six coffins in case any others die en route!

Isn't that cheerful? I still continue to like Mr. McGregor very much. He's nice. Mrs. Plumer has persuaded me to accompany her

---

6. Quoit, a ring of iron, rope, or rubber thrown in a game to encircle or land nearest to an upright peg.

and Mr. Archer across Japan by rail. We shall leave Yokohama in the morning and reach Kyoto in the evening, spend the night there, and go to Kobe the next morning or afternoon to catch our ship again. I have not communicated with the Osawas but shall hope to see them or Miss Denton or both. Either or both would be a treat to travelers.

We are a day late due to a storm, which delayed us two days ago. It was really a gorgeous affair; high waves breaking over the bow and spray clear across the ship. Mr. Archer and I watched it all one morning from the large porthole over the Purser's office on the main deck. He has as much enthusiasm over such foolishness as I have myself. I only hope the newspapers did not give lurid accounts of disaster or storm besetting us. No one was the least bit worried and only a few felt at all sick.

One night we were playing bridge in the social hall, that is Mrs. Howard, Dr. Monroe and Mrs. Hertig and I, and the orchestra came skidding over onto us; then I found myself mixed up with the saxophone and finally landed on the Victrola which is fastened down. Everyone completed similar journeys and we wished there had been a movie camera there to take a picture. It would have made a good comedy. I'll write more en route to Shanghai. This will catch the Jackson I think.

February 17, 1926 ~ Aboard *SS President Jefferson*

Dear Mother,

I am just now en route from Yokohama to Kobe by ship. All my interesting plans as outlined in a former letter seem to have exploded due to our ship not being in Yokohama long enough. We were delayed by rough sea and so arrived there at noon, pulled out at 4 p.m. Poor old Yokohama[7] is nearly as sad a wreck as before. I almost suspect they do not make a great effort to rebuild as they would if it were not a port city where they can round up plenty of sympathy. Certainly there has been little building in the last year and a half and they are still clearing away debris from some wrecked buildings.

I wonder how many years before there will be prosperity here. We tried to go to Kamakura where the large Buddha is situated in the

---

7. 1923 earthquake, which devastated Tokyo, the port city of Yokohama, surrounding prefectures

woods, but missed the train and found by waiting for the next one we'd be too late, so had lunch at the Tent Hotel in Yokohama, did a little window-shopping and let it go at that.

Coaling Station in Japan

"We" were Mrs. Plumer, Mrs. Howard, Mr. Archer and I. Mrs. Howard and the young Irishman do not get along very well so Mrs. Plumer and I are puzzling over how to rearrange our Kobe plans to leave the little lady out. It's a bit difficult but the three of us may dash up to Kyoto as we previously planned or per- haps stay for dinner in Kobe if by any chance the Osawas should have anyone in Kobe to meet me. We are due in Kobe at 3 this afternoon, and are scheduled to leave at midnight, which doesn't leave much time. I'll let you know from Shanghai just what did happen.

Mr. Archer, now known as Paddy, and I had a playful little contest this morning swinging as high as we could to see who could kick the ceiling flat-footed in the fewest pumps on the swing. Isn't that what you would call a delicate pastime? The picture of your long-legged daughter pumping the swing over the young gentleman's head was very merry. You would doubtless have been edified.

I am wondering what word I will receive in Shanghai of what my plans should be from there. I cannot work up any enthusiasm over dashing up to two last days of a nurses' conference in Nanking[8], hanging around another couple of days waiting for Auntie Nina. I should like

8. Now known as Nanjing and located in the lower Yangtze River drainage basin and Yangtze River Delta economic zone, Nanjing, historically, has been one of China's most important cities.

staying there until time to go right on upriver to Hankou[9]. It is possible there may be enough water in the Siang River to take a steamer to Changsha; otherwise, I will go by train.

I am enclosing a bill I found in my purse that should have gone to Mort Whitman right after the Christmas celebration at the church. Probably the Baptist office has sent another bill by this time. I hope so, as I did not realize I had this one so tenderly cherished.

We've been passing fleets of fishing junks which are wonderfully picturesque and quite a different shape and style from the Chinese. They also look better at a distance. It's a lovely bright sunny day so every white sail shows up particularly clearly.

I've mailed the letter to Miss Hirota, as I had no time to see her, of course.

February 19, 1926 ~ Aboard SS *President Jefferson*

Dear Mother,

This, our last day on board, is a lovely, clear, sunshiny day to make a good last impression. The jump from Japan to China is so short we shall find ourselves there before we realize what's happened. I took some extra candy boxes and the old plush coat down into the baggage room this morning and jammed them into the old "coffin" with much tugging and pushing. The baggage clerk thinks I'm crazy and I shall probably agree with him if the strap breaks on the wharf in Shanghai and scatters the possessions all over the pier.

I was disappointed to have so little time in Kobe; I could not get over to Kyoto to see the Osawas. We were scheduled to arrive at 5 p.m., which would have given enough time for the 2-hour trip each way and about four hours there, as we were to sail at midnight. Unfortunately we were late in arriving and did not get ashore until 5. I had written the Osawas that I would come over, bringing Mrs. Plumer and Mr. Archer in good Japanese style, so I went to their office in Kobe to tell them I would not be there.

I had the card of Mr. Yamasaki, who was a good little egg from the University of Pennsylvania some 15 years or so ago, I should guess.

---

9. Hankou was one of three cities whose merging formed modern-day Wuhan, the capital, now Hankow, of the Hubei province, China.

He was most courteous and served us coffee and cake in his office while calling Kyoto long distance. Finally, he got Yoshio, and I had an amusing conversation with him over the phone. He asked about all the family and wanted to know when Janet would be married. I had a terrible time trying to explain to him she wouldn't be married because it was broken off and finally repeated "never, never, never," which he understood. He remarked, "Why is it the Woolvertsons are so hard to marry?" Isn't that good? Then he had a lengthy conversation with Mr. Yamasaki, the result of which was the latter called a car, drove us to the falls just on the city outskirts, which are beautiful in rainy weather but dry now, and then to a temple, to Theatre Street, and finally to a restaurant, the same one where Fukiko took me in '24.

It is a perfect gem of a place built around a garden and spotlessly clean. We had a delicious sukiyaki dinner which is the meat and vegetables they cook on a brazier burning in the middle of the table, and which you eat with chopsticks, dipping the sizzling hot food into a bowl that contains a raw egg. They also gave us rice wine, hot and strong, lemonade and shrimp and fruit. It was delicious, much better than the cold fish we had in the summertime.

Mrs. Plumer reminds me very much of Miss Williams at college with out-of-date hats and ground-gripper shoes and a gentle, precise way of talking. She was a good sport and enthused over everything in an amusing way, turning to the little Japanese waitress and saying, "Really this is perfectly delicious." The waitresses would giggle and squeak at one another and Paddy Archer and I would nearly roll off the cushions with joy. Mr. Yamasaki and another man from the office were also amused, but very polite and complimented us on our dexterity with chopsticks, etc.

I really must confess I considered it a bit nervy to have imposed on the Osawas' good will to such an extent, but I truly had not expected to be entertained so lavishly at long distance. At the same time, I was glad to have been able to introduce my friends to a pleasant side of Japanese life and we certainly saw it there, whereas we didn't in Yokohama. They took us back to the ship at 9 o'clock and after I had taken off my coat and more or less resigned myself to the rest of the evening on board, Mrs. Plumer came around and said, "Now let's go ashore and have more good times, and it will be my treat" —all in a soft, gentle voice which sounded too inconsistent with the sentiment. We accepted the suggestion and rode about in rickshaws for another couple of hours, going along Theatre Street again and stopping at the hotel on the way back. A very successful evening, altogether. We were due to have sailed at midnight but there was so much cargo we didn't get away until two, which means I would have had time to go to Kobe after all, if I'd left late enough. It all worked out well anyhow.

I was vaccinated for smallpox this morning. I couldn't remember when I had had it done last so took this opportunity of guarding myself. They report cases from Shanghai but I guess there is always some there.

We had an informal performance in the Social Hall last night. The little Jewess en route to Manila is an acrobatic dancer by profession and though a little stale at present can do all sorts of fancy bending and rolling. I don't particularly admire it but I think interesting in small doses. She is so obviously doomed to a life of constant struggle against the fat, dumpy figure that I hand it to her for keeping fit so well.

Then a couple named Gravely who joined the ship in Yokohama gave us a "Charleston" dance exhibition, which was very neat indeed. They did it cleverly and well. Then Mr. Wooten, who is in the A.O. Line employ, sang for us. He has a marvelous tenor voice and I tried to play his accompaniment. I was so thrilled by his singing that it was hard to hit the notes. He has been sick and has not sung for a year and I'd certainly like to hear him when he's in trim. Six or seven years ago he was singing in a professional choir in New York. and offered a position in the Metropolitan Opera Company, which he refused. Doesn't it seem a shame a person with his talent shouldn't keep on developing it, instead of sticking to an old steamship job?

I rather thought I might get a letter or wire from the mission while in Japan but I guess they figured I don't need any encouragement or instructions, which is true enough.

I'm enclosing a stamp for Father's collection. He can call it Burns's if he wants to. Anyhow, it was a limited issue to honor the marriage of the Emperor's son. It will be choice in a few years if he guards it tenderly.

February 26, 1926 ~ Aboard *SS Kungwo*
Shanghai to Hankou

Dear Mother,

This ship furnishes peculiar stub pens, which almost serve to disguise a person's handwriting. I conclude the ruled paper is to guide the wandering hands of those who are returning from a vacation in Shanghai.

I've found my time quite full since reaching China. The last two days on the Jefferson were occupied with packing, washing and final preparations for leaving. Did I tell you we spent a whole day coming through the Inland Sea? The weather was a bit foggy so the distant hills were very hazy but we passed hundreds of islands of all sizes and whole fleets of picturesque fishing boats. The scenery reminded me somewhat of the San Juan Islands and Mrs. Hunt from Alaska said it was much like the trip up there.

I woke quite early and seeing land so near my porthole I got up for fear of missing something. It was before seven a.m. and the only time of day when the sun was out so I was not sorry. As a result, however, I went to sleep in the afternoon, asking Mrs. Plumer to call me if there was anything very choice to see. A terrible pounding on my door wakened me and in burst Paddy Archer just to tell me it was time for tea. Talk about informal characters! After tea, we three went way out on the bow where Mr. McGregor was in charge while we slowed down to let off the Japanese pilot.

Mrs. Plumer fluttered about after us like a poor hen chasing wandering chicks but we all enjoyed it.

It was snowing when we came to Shanghai early in the morning, an unusual occurrence. It was not heavy but enough to have covered everything with a coat of white. We landed so far down river, at the Dollar Line wharf, we had to change to a small launch to be taken up to the Customs. There, a Chinese from the Missionary Home met me and had my baggage passed with only a very casual mussing up of things in my trunk trays. Fortunately we arrived early enough for me to do my banking before noon, it being Saturday. I had a letter there from Nina Gage urging me to go up to the conference in Nanking. As I couldn't arrive before Sunday and the   vould be no meetings that

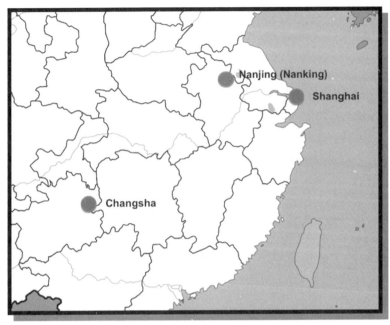

Nanjing:Changsha:Shanghai

day, I decided to go in time for the Monday sessions, leaving Shanghai Sunday evening.

The unusual old Missionary Home is still the same and Miss Spurling, the woman in charge, a great character. She gave me a very serious little talk on the dangers of traveling on the night train, as one girl had come to the Home a nervous wreck after a dreadful experience. She had been assigned to a cabin next to some drinking men and she heard them talking and then telling the porter to ask her to come in. The porter refused and she moved her cabin but she was in hysterics all the time. I thanked the woman for her solicitations and wanted to add that I questioned whether the poor girl was the sort of person who ought to travel anywhere alone.

I telephoned the American Consulate hoping to speak to Howard Bucknell but got Mr. Hamilton instead. He is Julia Fisher's husband, you know. I asked him whether Julia and Lucy would be home that afternoon and he was most cold and haughty and refused to commit himself even when I told him who I was. In about half an hour, Lucy called up and insisted I pack my bag immediately and they would come over to get me to stay with them. They have a Star car, which is called Rugby in the Orient. Their two-year-old son and the Hamiltons were with them and Max was most profuse in his apologies for his rude telephone conversation, insisting that he had thought it was Blanche Smith who lives in Shanghai and whom they all consider an awful bore. They live in adjoining apartments over the Consulate offices, very centrally located but not at all attractive. They have some lovely furniture and Howard has quite a collection of beautiful opium pipes, which had been confiscated during trials in the mixed court where he has presided.

Howard Jr. is a fat young person quite badly spoiled and speaking a weird sort of Pidgin English baby talk. Lucy will take him home on the return trip of the Jefferson and Howard will follow a month later for a six-month leave. They will return by way of Spain to visit her parents who are now stationed there in the Consular Service. It was mighty good to see them again.

Julia looks very bad in my opinion though Lucy says she is much better than she was a year ago. Her husband was sent to Hainan soon after they were married and she picked up dysentery somewhere en route. She is very colorless and thin and older-looking. Her mother rode on the ship as far as Victoria and I couldn't but think how lucky it is she did not come all the way.

They took me to a very poor film called *Barbara Ritchie* in which she never did have an "old gray head" and then out to the American Country Club where we had tea and played a game of table golf, a combination of golf and croquet, and pool, in which one shoots little rubber discs around with a cue. The clubhouse is rather new but attractive and with a large outdoor swimming pool which was closed and rather empty now.

We all went to the Hamiltons' place for dinner and I was most disgracefully sleepy during the evening so I went early to home and bed.

I had a tiffin[10] date with Mrs. Plumer and son Jim for Sunday so the Bucknells drove me out there and I met many people who were dashing in and out in the most informal manner. After tiffin a crowd of us went swimming in the pool, which is a feature of the apartment

---

10. A light meal.

house. It was not large but great fun. Jim has another Customs man living with him and there were two sisters named Roberts, one in a school in Shanghai and the other in a school in Wuchang[11] where the Kennicott girl taught. Friend Paddy and I were the last to emerge as might have been expected, being much occupied with swimming under water. He went back with me and the Bucknells to go to his hotel and pack up his things so he could move out with Jim the next day. I don't know what sort of crowded quarters they inhabit but they all seem happy. Mrs. Plumer can keep a watchful eye on them to see they behave!

I met Mrs. Hooker at the Missionary Home for tiffin. It seems she is not a bit popular with the Beamans, who do the business part of the Home as they were responsible for putting her out from there. We were, therefore, given a table to ourselves in the sitting room, which was, I suppose, a great insult, but which pleased us immensely as it meant we could talk uninterruptedly. She had been up country and fell during a very dark night spraining her right wrist. She was wearing it in a sling and feeling quite uncomfortable with it. Otherwise she seems quite happy but misses her boys who distress her by failing to write. Did you ever hear of such a thing? She had sent a card to the boat for me by a Mrs. Hill of Seattle who was going to meet a man also on the Jefferson. I never saw him, though someone told me I was being paged. Mrs. Hooker talks of going to Seattle on her vacation this summer but is not certain about it yet.

My trip up to Nanking was quite uneventful. I had a fairly comfortable berth and managed to keep warm enough by wearing my kimono to bed. There were no drinking men, or women either, and we arrived just on time. It was most chilly and I nearly froze being driven the five miles out to Nanking University in a terribly stylish sort of "Victoria." They seem the favorite vehicles and a poor scrawny horse drew it, which must be unusually tough.

I was assigned to the Reisner home. He teaches Agriculture and knows Dwight both from China and New Haven. His wife is very pleasant, though I saw little of her as she developed tonsillitis on Monday evening and came down to no more meals. They have children 10, 7

11. Wuchang is located on the south bank of the Yangtze River (Chang Jiang) at the confluence of the Han River, opposite Hankow and Hanyang

and 5 who were lots of fun but have the most atrocious table manners I've seen for some time.

That day's session at the conference had already begun so I sneaked into a back seat of the chapel, where the meetings were held. Miss Gage was on the platform and wigwagged when she saw me. I hardly knew her as she had on the most terrible hat. I remember blushing for her when she had it on in the fall of '24 and here she is still wearing it. I think there's going to be an unintentional but beneficial fire in her house some day!

February 28, 1926 ~ Hankou

Dear Mother,

I had a lengthy epistle started to you I was going to finish here in Hankou, but it has gone merrily on to Changsha and here am I. The answer is a situation, which peeves me more each time I think of it. I arrived yesterday afternoon by boat and took in tow the two women and two men nurses—Chinese—who had also been at the conference. The latter two arranged about baggage and were to transfer it to the ferry and then we would cross the river to the train. They stayed to escort it and we waited at the ferry until too late to get to the train and still they did not appear and I haven't seen them to this moment. I conclude they took the baggage and have gone to Changsha but why they didn't join us I don't know yet. The worst is, the pass they had was for themselves and the two women nurses whose fares I shall have to pay now I suppose. My pass is still good. Some class, I'd say, traveling on a pass. I got it through Dr. Yen.

I haven't seen anyone in Hankou except those at the C and A Mission Home where I'm staying. Mrs. Harvey has asked about Dwight and cousin Harold [business manager for the family]. Mrs. Braun, who knows Uncle Everett's family, is in Kuling.[12] I understand.

By tomorrow noon I'll be in Changsha again and glad to have my traveling done, though I've enjoyed it ever so much and feel fine. It's lucky as one nurse, Miss Beebe, has been sick and is now on four-hour duty and Lisa Gage is not back yet from Shanghai.

---

12. Kuling: Lushan District is a district in Jiujiang, Jiangxi, China.

Dr. Hume and family have gone to Europe. No one seems to know why or for how long, but there is a rumor there may be another president next year.

I'll let you know more about it after I arrive at the source of information.

Hankow/Wuhan:Changsha:
Shanghai:Beijing

Hsiang-Ya Medical College

March 2, 1926 ~ Changsha

Dear Mother,

The conference in Nanking was the slowest moving performance, as everything was translated several times into English or Chinese as the case might be. Then too they discussed all sorts of trivial things. The sessions began at 8:30 a.m., lasted until noon, then again from 2:00 p.m. to 4:00 or later, and again from 8 p.m. until 9 or 10. That is an awful dose for anybody. Fortunately, the Chinese are the sort of people who adore the long-stand parties and they didn't mind a bit though I found it awfully tiresome to say the least.

One day I went to the American Consulate and had tea with Gordon Burke. He has not changed at all. I've heard since that he is engaged and will be married in June to a girl in the Christian Mission there. Another day we all went for tea to Ginling College[13]. They have a new place with seven buildings, all built at the same time, in the same attractive style. I saw the plans in '22 and was interested to see the finished product. On Wednesday we, from Changsha, were invited to tea with Dr. Jen, a graduate of the local Medical School.

The food was marvelous, but I committed the *faux pas* of being unable to finish my second bowl of rice. I was too full and furthermore everyone else had finished before me, strange to say! I hoped they would think my bad manners were due to my long absence from China. I asked Dr. Jen if he knew the Kiang family and explained how I knew them through my parents.

So after lunch this Miss Golich conducted me to her school which is a Methodist affair and I met Mr. Kiang. He wished to be remembered to you both and Dwight. He took me to his house and I met another son who is a junior at Nanking University and a fine-looking boy. Mrs. Kiang was ill so I didn't see her. The son who is a Dr. expects to go to Peking next year and they hope the daughter who is also an M.D. now in France will be there too. They are a bright family and I was much interested in meeting Mr. Kiang.

---

13. Ginling College (aka Ginling Women's University and Ginling Women's College of Arts and Sciences) was a Christian university (founded 1913) in Nanjing, China. It was the first Chinese university to issue bachelor's degrees to women.

I had to get up about 5 a.m. the next day as the boat from Shanghai upriver often comes in and goes out early depending on the water. Miss Zink and I met on the boat that came by about 7:30 and had a good trip up. She is a very pleasant young woman, a graduate of a hospital in Kansas. She has been doing TB work in Colorado and is now in a Presbyterian Mission in Changteh[14], I had a stateroom with the Miss Roberts I had met in Shanghai who was on her way back to her school in Wuchang[15]. Wasn't it a queer coincidence? It seemed strange to have the Yangtze River[16] so low. When I've been on it before it has been at full water but now we are so far below the riverbank level in places that we couldn't see the fields over the edge. Formerly, the water has been all over the fields and we seemed in the middle of a lake but this time we edged back and forth from bank to bank following the channel and taking constant soundings.

I wrote how we became separated in Hankou and it seems the men did cross the river with the baggage so we followed the next day. It was slightly chilly at night though I had my heavy coat. I let the little nurse use it part-time so we didn't entirely freeze. I had chocolate and a tin of crackers and we ate some Chinese chow so we were not hungry at least. No one met us so I went right away to the Branch home[17] where I am to stay until summer.

They seem little changed but the youngsters have grown a lot. The sister of John Carter Vincent, the one who was so crazy about Eleanor Keller, is living at the Branches' also. It is the old Gage house but is all disguised in giddy cretonne[18] and pink lampshades and all sorts of do-dads which Pope adores. She has noisy taste in furnishings but is a hospitable soul.

---

14. Now known as Changde, a city in the north of Hunan Province, China.

15. Wuchang is located on the south bank of the Yangtze River (Chang Jiang) at its confluence with the Han River.

16. The Yangtze, Yangzi is the longest river in Asia, and third longest in the world. It flows for 3,988 miles from the glaciers on the Tibetan Plateau.

17. Dr. Branch is Hospital Superintendent.

18. A heavy cotton, linen, or rayon fabric, usually printed with a colorful design. Use: upholstery.

We went to the Mission meeting last night, as supper and meeting of all the missions in Changsha. I saw many people I know and it was great fun.

Charlie Keller walked home with me. He is fatter than before, otherwise the same cheery person apparently. It's fine to be here at last and find everyone and everything well and happy. I think it will be a good spring.

I was glad to get your letter telling of Emmy Lou's wedding. It must have been a hectic affair. I can imagine what a wreck Mrs. Howard is. Poor soul.

I hope you can dispose of the rugs lucratively but I don't know what to suggest about the linen. I suppose Dwight has not mentioned it again. All my possessions came through except the record "Dinah" by the Revelers, which is cracked. It still plays all right but I would like to have another record of it some time when you are sending things to me. I shall have plenty of letters to write when I am better settled. I hope Eunice and Frank are taking good care of you at home and Mrs. Schively of Dad at the office. I think E.L. is a bit late in his suggestion of Brad White and matrimony. They should have supplied encouragement some time ago.

March 9, 1926 ~ Changsha

Dear Mother,

I have now been back here on duty for a week and it almost begins to seem like a long time. I still cannot realize, occasionally, that I am here, but as I never quite got over the feeling all the time I was out here before, I am not surprised at it now. Everyone is very cordial and though I have not discovered anyone I should care to have as a very bosom friend, they are all dreary and nice. The two nurses are good eggs. Lisa Norelius or Jess is the more efficient. Dr. Branch says that she is just a big comfortable Swede, which is a good description if she is a Swede. Nell Beebe lacks a sense of humor and has a terrible complexion. She has been ill all winter with amoebic dysentery but is better now and is on four-hour duty. Lisa Gage is not at all well I should say though she carries on about the same. She doesn't do much ward work and I certainly can't blame her as she has others to do it and besides I think she may have lost heart over it a bit since her year at home when the nurses had a strike and more or less went to pieces. I do think their morale has changed. They have orderlies on the wards, sort of dignified coolies whom the nurses get to do many things they should do themselves.

Consequently they are not really busy enough.

I had dinner with Miss Gage the other night and she told me that when she heard how short of funds they were last spring she resigned, but they did not accept her resignation.

Changsha:Shanghai:Beijing

Her final decision peeved her family very much, she says. I think in a way it is too bad that she didn't stay home, as she is not as robust as she was and is dieting all the time and looks not well, but she is doubtless happier here. She has a lot of correspondence regarding the International Council of Nurses of which she is now President, and with the prospect of the convention of same here in Peking in 1929. It seems a long way off but considering the slowness of mails it is not too early to begin planning.

The Mission had a party last night with yours truly as honored guest, so to speak. They have had these Mission get-togethers several times this year and they are great fun—Chinese and foreign staff members. We had a cafeteria supper and then very funny entertainment consisting of "Crayon Portraits." It would be a good stunt for a New Year's party. The music and words came out in a copy of *Life* for July 8, I think it was 1925. The words describe the people from the family album. Charlie Keller sang the words and the people appeared in the doorway in a frame of gilt. Louise Farnam[19] in a high-necked lace blouse was sister "oft by wicked traveling men betrayed," Neil Sanford, brother Roscoe ruined at the "racetrack," Dr. Branch, "Uncle who went to the Klondike," etc. The costuming was wonderful and I chortled loudly as did everyone else, so they had to show it all over a second time. After everyone else went home, I lingered at the Fosters', where the party was held, and Charlie and his roommate Hutchins and the Fosters and I sang lustily for an hour or so

Dr. Louise Farnam
(Records of the Yale-China Association, 1900-1979 [inclusive]. Manuscripts & Archives, Yale University)

longer. It was good fun. The Branches went home and played bridge with the Rollins. They are terrible bridge fiends. I like it in smaller doses.

I am still living at the Branch home in an atmosphere of coal gas and heat, which is oppressive. I didn't know what was the matter on Saturday when I had a headache and felt dopey until I realized it was the terrible furnace smell. So Sunday I took myself off for a long walk. No one else seemed available so I lit off along a stone highway, which joins our Siang River. It is about three miles and was a good morning for walking.

The only trouble was that it was very muddy and I had to keep my eyes fixed on the road rather than about in the trees and hills. At the road's end is a high stone arch. I sat on the wall and chatted with the ragamuffins there assembled and had four lusty dogs try to scare the

---

19. Louise Farnam was one of the first women admitted to the Yale School of Medicine. Farnam graduated first in her class. She taught and practiced medicine for ten years in China.

wits out of me at once. They are horrid animals that bark and growl in a fierce way but are great cowards when confronted with a stick. I tried to take a short cut home but it proved to be a long cut, which was interesting but long. I met a little native brother of whom I asked the way, to be conversational, so we ambled back along the last mile of railroad track together; he laboring under the delusion that he was guiding and me fearing he would expect or demand coppers as a reward for services rendered.

There is something very charming in the rolling hills and narrow roads around here I think. There are considerable numbers of trees to give shade—bamboo and pines, but not so large or lofty as to obscure the territorial view and streams beyond when one is on top of a knoll. I like our mountain type immensely but this is rather comforting too.

In the afternoon I went to church with Dr. Branch and young daughter Anne. There I saw a number of people I had not previously encountered. They all seemed glad to see me and the women had on the most terrible looking hats imaginable.

Hilda Yen and her cousin had been in for tea. The former is still here and as attractive as ever. She is not awfully happy or reconciled to staying here indefinitely but manages to keep up with frequent trips to Hankou, Peking or Shanghai. She hopes to go to London this year with W. W. Yen if he is sent there from Peking. She has had a hard time trying to adjust to changes from America. She is doing secretarial work in the Hsiang-Ya Hospital in Clarice's place, though she doesn't know shorthand and is not too good at the typewriter. Her clothes are lovely in quite the latest Chinese style with a very long skirt. It looks queer beside our short clothes.

March 12, 1926 ~ Changsha

Dear Mother,

Very interesting political questions are wafting about these days. Zhao Heng-ti,[20] our governor, is about to go. I don't know just why but the impression seems to be that he is weary of his labors, has made a

---

20. Zhao Heng-ti was one-time governor of Hunan Province who became commander-in-chief of Hunan in 1920 but was expelled by revolutionary comrades, members of the Chinese Communist Party.

General Zhao Hengti
(Wikipedia)

General Wu Pei' fu
(Wikipedia)

good sum from squeeze, and believes in getting out while the times are peaceful. A man named Tang from south of here—Henchow[21], will take his place. It is rumored that Tang is a very Red sort of person and opposed to General Wu P`ei-fu[22], so I don't know what that means. If General Wu were not so busy in the North he would probably send troops here to support his friend Chao to keep the province in his control. Tang represents Canton interests, as I understand it. Dr. Yen is fortunately a good friend of his, so we shall probably not be molested.

I went into the city last night to Miss Hasenpflug's to dinner and Hilda Yen backed out at the last minute because it was threatened the city would be under martial law. I met no one at all and was not questioned anywhere though I passed by the Governor's *yamen*[23]. We had a lovely dinner, but left soon afterward—at 10 o'clock—having received the password. It consisted of two syllables, "koo-ghin," said in a high tone. When asked for it one says the first word and if asked again whispers the second so that all the people on the street will not hear. Unfortunately, no one even looked at us so the password was wasted.

---

21. Now known as Hengyang, a city south of Changsha.

22. Wu P`ei-fu was a major participant in the wars between the warlords who dominated Republican China from 1916 to 1927.

23. Yamen is a local bureaucrat or mandarin's office and residence.

A rather amusing thing occurred today. One of the medical students, now an intern from Soochow[24], is a long, lanky person, a good tennis player, and very much interested in his work too. An obstetrical patient came in with a history of a baby born the night before, and she had an old dirty coolie shoe tied onto the placenta cord, which was retained. They found that she had excessive fluid and a twin, quite premature and apparently dead. The doctor in charge left when the patient was returned to the ward, but this medical student named Liu happened to spy the baby in the garbage bucket and fished it out and after an hour had successfully restored it to life. Then, feeling that as everyone else had deserted it, that it belonged to him, he carefully wrapped it up in blankets, put a wad of cotton on its head and put it in a chair in one resident's room, and then went off to play tennis!

The first I knew of it was the resident coming to tell me there was a baby in his room. Dr. Liu had covered the chair with a gown and pinned on a sign, "Be careful! My baby in here!" I put an electric light inside to keep it warm when I found out about it and then we moved it to the babies' nursery.

Just as I was ready to go off duty, Dr. Liu came back and we went to see about the infant, finding him very blue, occasionally crying and looking about 99 years old as preemie babies usually do. We labored over the poor thing for another hour, but he finally died as we had expected and we each went back home for dinner. The whole thing was quite typical of this student, which is a very hopeful sign, as most are not so vitally interested in the patients' welfare, particularly a case like that. It was not even on his service.

We have also a very wild-haired Pole here, a pastry cook, etc., from Hong Kong who came here under the impression that it was a great metropolis and was robbed by a Russian and sent into the cold world knee-deep in water, etc., until his feet froze and he came here a sad wreck with gangrene of his toes. He tells his story in a dramatic manner that scares the Chinese nurses a bit. He asked me for 20¢ for stamps and cigarettes and when I gave it to him he nearly fell out of bed in his eagerness to seize and kiss my hand. Needless to say, that amazed the Chinese also.

---

24. Now known as Suzhou.

I have hardly seen Charlie Keller, but he seems calm and placid and quite fat and with a fat man's walk. He seems to have the same rating with the community as before.

The Harvey child who was so sick is still a very puny specimen. I see her occasionally ambling around the campus. I ask how she is and she is apt to say, "I was a little sick yesterday" in a poor pathetic voice. She is hardly what one would call robust but is evidently better than before.

I am rather eager to get into another house, not that I'm uncomfortable where I am but it is a bit crowded and I do not feel free to ask guests there and am more or less obliged to be one of the family when there are people there or when the Branches are asked out, I am included more from duty I fear than choice sometimes. For the present it is very pleasant, however … foreign mail this week brought letters from home and a copy of one from Jo, also one from Gladys Rose telling of the death of Edith Riley's father. He was quite old, well over 70, I should say. I was glad to receive the check for $35 which I am depositing in Mex. Did I tell you my salary began January first so on the end of this month I will receive $500 Mex, a very neat beginning toward savings. I shall be interested to see if Miss Hunter wants more rugs. If they can be sold readily there is good profit in them. When those you have are disposed of I should like to hand the Fosters a little *cumsha*[25] for the trouble they took in having them made here. I have not yet arranged for the "Pilgrim Bed" as there are no particularly interesting patients for it and there is no immediate need for the money. I'll attend to it one day.

I hope Susan is quite well. Today is Edwin's birthday. I hope he is having a grand time. I've had lumbago this week. My Kingdom for the Static, eh what?

I'm quite all right now.

March 17, 1926 ~ Changsha

Dear Mother,

I am recovering from another attack of lumbago. I have received the sympathy of Dr. Branch who has it occasionally, also that of young

---

25. Cumsha (Cumshaw) a bribe, present or bonus; -- originally applied to that paid on ships which entered the port of Canton.   S. Wells Williams. [1913 Webster]

John Carter Vincent who by the way is Eleanor Keller's friend. We are
going to put in an application for a place in the Old Folks Home and
the first one to get there will put in a reservation for the other. I am
using the electric baking machine. It is just a dome-like affair with
electric globes in the inside but does good work. As long as I keep on
my feet I'm all right but the rising up from a chair is painful. Ask Dad
if he knows I am wearing the corset I bought just before leaving home
and it is quite comfortable for the back.

Will you ask Dad if there is any other metal than block tin that
can be used on the diathermy[26] machine? If I had known they had a
small machine out here I would have bought tin for them at home. We
can have brass electrodes made of course, and pewter or copper if they
would serve. We could make up in quantity at any rate, as any would
be cheaper than having it sent from home.

Also, how about Dad sending *Northwest Medicine* out here to the
Medical School library? I don't know what arrangements could be made
about the subscription price but it would be a good addition to their supply. I was asking Dr. Branch if he knew about brother Scott for instance,
and told him about Dr. Coffee's articles on transplanting ureters and that
all that wealth of information was included in Papa's paper.

(*Note: 1926 – 1928 encompassed what later became known as
"The Northern Expedition," a military campaign led by the Kuomintang
[KMT] from 1926 to 1928. Its main objective was to unify China under
the Kuomintang banner by ending the rule of local warlords. It led to
the Beiyang government's demise; and, the Chinese 1928 reunification.
Harriet was right in the middle of conflict as the warring armies moved
up and down the Siang River Valley.*)

There is a very interesting political situation here now, though
no one seems to know just what is going on. One thing certain is that
Chao Heng-ti [27] (Zhao Heng-ti), the governor, has left. Why he has

---

26. Diathermy The production of heat in body tissues by electric currents, for therapeutic
purposes.

27. Zhao Heng-ti, a general and warlord of Hunan during the Warlord Era. In 1922, he was
promoted to commander of the New Xiang Army of the Beiyang Government. As a trusted
subordinate of Tan Yankai, he fought with Tan in supporting General Wu Pei-fu, later forcing
Tan's resignation from the governorship of Hunan in November 1920. Zhao Heng-ti became
the military governor of Hunan from 1920 to March 1926.

left is another matter. The impression seems to be there will be some sort of trouble somewhere between the southern Red element and the northern troops some time in the future. Hunan is, of course, a pathway for the troops either way as is Kaingsi[28], so each side likes to have the power here.

Chao is friendly with the North—General Wu P`ei-fu to be exact—and they say that General Wu told him if he would stay, that he, General Wu, would send troops to help him defend his position. On the other hand, it is also said that Chao has gone to get together with General Wu and dope out some policy because the southerners would probably come and kick him out if he didn't get out more peacefully. Anyhow there was not the slightest sign of trouble anywhere and Chao went away three days before the new man, Tan, came in, and all went on as before. The only exception that I have heard about is that when Chao walked out, the Reds went and appropriated his Yamen and announced that no place in the city could be more appropriate for their purposes. Fortunately, Dr. Yen is a great friend of Tan so that we ought to have no trouble with the new administration. No one knows just how much city taxes went out with Chao but he probably has enough to live comfortably for the rest of his life, and I cannot blame him for getting out with it intact rather than wasting it on military expenditures.

It has been raining almost all the time since I came. We have a few days of rain and then maybe one of bright weather and then rain again. The river has risen way up so the gunboats have exchanged, an American going out and a British coming in. The American left one man behind in our care with pneumonia. Fortunately he is much better and will be ready to leave in another week. The Chinese are holding their breath wondering when the rain will cease and whether it will ruin the rice crop again this season.

The price of rice has gone up about a thousand percent in the last few years and there must be much suffering in the outlying districts as well as in the cities. It is hard to know what to think about it. It is so obvious there has been, and is, terrible profiteering in the matter of exporting rice and the squeeze from the high prices, and then they use the foreigners' money to buy more rice to give away to the poor

28. Jiangxi, a southern province

starving refugees. They come into the city in swarms and are given rice at the stations established for that purpose and then load themselves into the trains, on top as well as inside and go off again. I don't know where they go and what they do when they get there but they probably turn around and come back again. It is a tough situation.

Everything in the mission seems calm and cool, almost too much so. They need a bit of stirring up in some quarters but it is more comfortable.

The favorite indoor sport seems to be bridge, especially in this household. For that reason, as well as to have some relief from the crowd in this house and to be more independent, I should like to move into the Humes's house. It would be nicer for me in many ways, and a relief from the crowd in this house. So far I have not had anyone enthusiastic over the prospect of moving there with me, but I have hopes. We have had much fun about it and I tell them that I have decided to go there and rent out furnished rooms to any one. Two bachelors from town say they will come out and take rooms and Hilda Yen says she thinks it is a fine idea.

I wrote to Mrs. Pontius yesterday, news that can be broadcasted with no harm. I have told her I have the money from the church still intact. As I told her, the Hsiang-Ya Hospital is not at all full and there are no deserving cases in right now. I shall let them know that I have the money and if something does turn up we can apply the money there. I have thought of giving some to the nurses to fix up their tennis court and buy balls. They have so little planned for them off duty; a lot of encouragement and help in any of their projects [such as] $10 Mex from the sum, would help them a lot and would leave plenty for the bed. I have not quite decided yet about it.

I trust you have received my letters all right, which I have written along the way since I arrived here. I have had another from Jo but no mention regarding sale of linen. Did I tell you that I am receiving salary from the first of January so shall send a check to the Swatow people for the linen and get that off my chest, and keep any money I may receive in the future, or just hang onto the linen itself? I think it is not a bad investment for the future.

March 23, 1926 ~ Changsha

Dear Mother,

We had mail on Sunday from America that was very nice. I heard from home and Elizabeth Henry; also from Clarice. Hank tells the various bits of news of our friends, but does not mention that young Conklin is keeping her doorstep warm. Is it possible that that little seed did not take root? She seems to be consoling herself with the man from the bank whom I met at Marguerite Han's just before I left home; that is, as much as is possible for her which is not much. She is really very amusing on the subject.

I have been fairly busy the past week finding out how things in the hospital are not as they once were, and how many should be jacked up. The strike in the nursing school during the fall after I left did rather serious things to the male nurses' efficiency. They had to get orderlies to do a great deal of bell-answering and that sort of thing. Of course, it has meant the nurses put a great deal off on them which they ought to recognize as purely nursing work. It is very hard to draw distinctions, and then to get the nurses to follow them, particularly as there are so few nurses—about 20 where there used to be 55.

Another unfortunate feature is that they continue to spit blood at intervals, one of them doing so today, and then having to go to bed for goodness knows how long. Just the same, I do like it and am extremely fond of all of them and the other Chinese in the office and on the staff. I flatter myself that I get along well with them and had the nerve to repeat to my family that I have been told by different nurses and interns that they are quite certain the whole trouble would have been settled peacefully and amicably without the loss of nurses if Miss Gage or I had been here.

Helen Brundage did the best she could, but had the unfortunate faculty of antagonizing the Chinese. I have been rather surprised to find the altogether friendly attitude of all the Chinese, quite the same or more so than when I was here before. On the streets the kids yell "foreign devil" at us, but that is nothing new. I used to hear this before. Certainly I could not ask for a more peaceful and quiet spot than this. I've never even been challenged in the street and asked for the password. That is disappointing! After the excitement of the good old

USA, where they could stage a few first-class murders or a diamond holdup or something like that on most any well-behaved citizen, this place is really tame.

There are still many famine refugees in the city, going in and coming out, and as we rode home from the Heinrichsons' last night we passed ever so many of them parked in dark doorways in heaps of rags and humanity, trying to get some sleep and succeeding rather well to judge from the sounds and general appearance of lifelessness.

I had Sunday off this last week and had been invited to spend the weekend with Gladys Trivetta Box, who was the nurse here before and was married last fall. Her husband had gone on an up-country trip so she was alone. She was spending the night over here on Friday and early Saturday they sent word for her to come home because her house was on fire. She hastened home to find the coolie had, the night before—contrary to her four-times-repeated instructions—forgotten and lit the fire in the kitchen stove. After a few hours, he remembered, so he raked out the coals quite hastily and put them in the coal box with the unburned coal and then went to bed, until five in the morning when the servants were all awakened by the smell of smoke.

He naively remarked that he had noticed the coals from the stove were not very alive. The kitchen smoldered quietly until the floor burned through, lowering the kitchen stove leg into the room below and blistering all the paint and varnish and making an awful mess. Needless to say, we did not go there for the night.

I went with the Branches and Margaret Vincent to the Valpys' for a curry tiffin Saturday noon. It was delightful and the little snooze, which it seems is the proper style afterward, was equally enjoyable.

That done, I went with the Valpys to the Club on the island and dressed for dinner, continuing to Ratti's home. He is a little critter in the shipping company here, formerly known by Jane as "that little rat named Runti." Just the same he is a cordial soul and we had a very friendly dinner party there. It was to honor his successor named Feely who had just come up from Shanghai with his wife.

She and I did not play bridge after dinner so sat and talked for about three hours. It does not sound very exciting but was very agreeable, as she is a charming person about my age brought up in Shanghai and feeling that she had come to the end of the world in coming to Changsha. I wonder how she will get along with the business community not playing bridge, as most of them are friends, but I also think that if there is so charming a person about who does not care for cards, the others who do not care for it either will develop interests in some other form of sport. I don't know just what. Then too the annual transfers are going on and the entire community is being reorganized, and sent home, and fired, and whatnot. I do hope to see more of Mrs. Feely as she impressed me as a good scout and yet a person with much weight above the ears.

Sunday I went with Hilda Yen and her cousin and Margaret to tiffin with the APC[29] Junior mess. They have moved to the island's end into a rather pleasant house in somewhat poor surroundings. After tiffin we all set out to walk to Yolo-san [30], the mountain, and have tea. I never struck such a poor, washed-out crowd of hikers in my life. They were always wanting to rest and all sank entirely mired in a time out, and when we did finally reach the temple, nearly at the top, they sat down in a state of utter exhaustion, called for food and drink, and disregarded my suggestion that we should climb higher and admire the view, leap from crag to crag and whatnot. I am having a good time out of it anyhow, having a good chance to size up the various people here, what they are like, what they like to do, and all that.

The Friday Club met here last week and was addressed by Wally Tyng, the Episcopal Mission head. He is the one who a few years ago started to write the third part to the Bible. He thought the Old Testament was written for God, the New for Christ, and so he was writing the third for the Holy Ghost. He seems to have recovered from that, but is odd in spots. He talked last week on "personality," reviewing church history in a way and making diagrams of the Trinity, and using such technical language that hardly any of us poor benighted lay members knew what he was raving about. The discussion afterward was not very lively, because so few did understand or could follow it.

29. Asiatic Petroleum Company—Shell Transport and Royal Dutch were originally competitors. In 1903, they agreed to establish a joint marketing company for the Far East operations. The Asiatic Petroleum Company was thus incorporated in London.

30. Now known as Yuelu Mountain Scenic Area consisting of hills, pinnacles, rivers, lakes, a variety of species, flora and fauna, a cultural historic site and revolutionary monuments.

Mrs. Branch had a letter from Jane the other day that was crazy as anything. She passed it around to others to read and Louise Farnam was quite depressed over it feeling that it indicated the poor girl is really losing her mind. It was quite dippy. She raved at great length about her travels in Italy, bringing in poetic references to sunsets over the hills, and the flavor of wine presses and a courtly gray-haired count who kissed her hand, and all that sort of thing. Then she goes on to rave about how no one at home has anything intelligent to talk about and how it is seldom, but occasionally refreshing, that she gets some kindred souls together of a Sunday evening to talk about really good music and whatnot.

She refers to Dr. Farnam as "Louisa, the stainless maiden physician," and to me as "the redoubtable Hat, invincible in love and the training of nurses," which is, I think, proof of her unbalanced state. I tell them that it is nothing new, but just so happens they have never been in a position of sufficient distance to be favored by her letters before. Have you seen anything of her?

By the way, while I think of it, you asked about what I meant by saying that "Jane would pay duty" on the rugs. That was in case she took the whole lot, as she at one time insinuated that she would. That was to be one way of disposing of them if you did not care to have them on your hands. Apparently she does not care to take them, or did not care to. She talked at one time of going into business and told of how her old boss in Seattle was willing and eager to finance it, and there was a man here willing to do this end of it. I have not heard from her at all; so conclude that it was idle talk, which I might have expected.

I have bought an elegant kite for Burns, and am having the carpenter make a box for it. I don't know what the postage will be, but if it goes through all right it will be a wonderful addition to the whole neighborhood's entertainment. It is a centipede with a big flat face and mouth on the front and then numerous discs of gradually decreasing size joined with string, making the whole thing about 20 feet long when out to full size. Each disc has long bamboo feelers on each side with whiskers on the end. I saw one of them flying on Saturday and it was wiggling and squirming in the sky just like a real great big caterpillar. If they do not understand how to get it up at Eunice's, they should call in Harold. It takes three or four people holding it to get it up. I would suggest doing it on the University campus. At least they would have an audience I think. Perhaps brother Chang or Frank would assist.

How is Frank? Still painting I suppose. Be sure that he does not work so hard that he gets bad marks like B's in his studies. Is he talking of going to the cannery again this summer or will he go to summer school?

Did I tell you that I left my steamer rug on the ship when I arrived at Shanghai? I am glad that I did in that it meant less baggage to carry, though I would have been glad to have it on the train from Hankou to Changsha. However, I wrote the steamer Purser and asked him to send it to me and it arrived today. I consider myself fortunate as it was not unlike the regular ship kind and it would have been quite possible for the deck boy to swipe it.

Today was a lovely spring day and it begins to look as though we are in for some good sunshine again. I have had my old uniforms made over with the belt removed and the skirt put up higher onto the waist with a yoke. Then I wear a loose belt and it is ever so much more comfortable and better-looking. It took the house tailor two days, which will mean $1.20 for the job. When I recover from that expenditure, which is about 65¢ US money, I shall call the outside tailor to turn my camel's hair suit. Then I'll be set for spring, in or out.

The news about Mrs. Landes[31] was most gratifying and I shall be curious to hear how the finals come out. I remember the predictions that she would be elected and the City Manager would also pass so that she would never really serve a term as mayor. I'll be eager to hear the outcome of it all.

Too bad you cannot change administrations as easily as they have just done here. One man walks out and the other walks in a few days later. The Communists took over the Governor's Yamen in the interim but have since been ousted. No one seems to know just where old Chao, the previous Governor, is now or what he plans to do. Probably, as Jan said about the US and the Philippines, "What will Uncle Sam do about

---

31. Mrs Bertha Landes was a strong willed reformer City Manager who won 1926 election and later earned kudos for "Driving Out Bandits and Bootleggers," *The Star*, February 19, 1928

the Philippines? Probably he will do as he pleases." That is doubtless what Chao will do.

I'm glad my pictures were satisfactory. I don't particularly care about having any sent out here, but I would like to see the newspaper print of it to give me an idea of what they look like. I blush to say the nurses still have the old one I sent from White Plains, and I have asked them to take it down now that I am here in person, but they probably will cling to it. In fact, one of them insinuated they were thinking of having mine and Miss Gage's enlarged. Wouldn't that be wonderful, particularly if they would only have them done in silk embroidery! What a thought!

March 30, 1926 ~ Changsha

Dear Mother,

I've been here almost a month now and it seems at least that. It's quite astonishing how easily and quickly I have fallen into hospital routine. I hate not having a home of my own or being a part of a "mess" where I can feel free to ask whom I like when I please. Instead I am living with the Dr.'s family who took out my appendix in "days of yore."

He is rather a good egg, but not the sort who would inspire me at least to break up a happy home. He has a clever line, but a very crude sense of humor with a medical tinge that makes it racy, to say the least. His wife is a redheaded person with a good heart but a rather common nature, I have always thought. She is always telling us about the wealth of her sister or "Aunt Carrie" or someone else and adores discussions of clothes, jewels, servants, etc. However, she's a good scout and has treated me with hospitality since I came back.

Still, I would not live there if I could find a place to keep house with a kindred soul or two. The two main difficulties are there are no spare houses except a huge one near which I now live and no kindred souls this side of the briny deep. If my luck is better, I may find some of each before another year.

To give you an idea of my dissipations, last Thursday a tea dance, which I did not attend; Saturday a curry tiffin with the Valpys—railroad people living a mile or so from here; a short snooze all over the house afterward; then home just too late to see a football game with tea afterward; then to a dinner and dance at the home of Miss Gage. Saturday I went on the "trolley"—polite name for the handcar that belongs to the Valpys—to a nearby mountain to pick azaleas. It was lovely and warm with just enough breeze but not enough flowers, sad to say.

They used to be thick there, but the drought last summer just about finished them. "We" were John Carter Vincent, the man who vamped Eleanor Keller away from her husband, his sister who is visiting at the Branches where I stay, and Pa Valpy who owns the railroad, as it were. I went to church like a good Italian girl and then back to the Valpys' for dinner.

The Italian gunboat Captain was there, a Mr. Mariano whom Margaret Vincent quite successfully vamped to the point of his offering to light her cigarette at his burning heart! Isn't that choice?

Everyone had the most powerful cocktails imaginable beforehand and four of them spent quite a time discussing the punctuation of "that that is." Noisy? My goodness! After dinner, which Mrs. Valpy called a 'quiet farm supper,' we had hymn singing and then other singing and then good-byes.

Jane writes pathetically how she misses the Valpys. They are a good pair, but really awfully small and 2 x 4 in many ways. However, it takes all kinds to make a world, I've been told.

This week I go out to dinner Wednesday, Thursday, and Saturday with another tea dance at the Club Thursday afternoon. It's a crazy lightheaded way to spend one's time and I'm not so dippy about it as I once was. My chief idea in the gay life now is to meet the various people and see if I can discover a kindred spirit. I think I found one in Mrs. Feely, whose husband is the representative of a local steamship line. She is a Shanghai girl of about my age I should guess, is a good sport, a fair amount of brains, and like myself—and strange to say—does not play bridge. There are a few of that kind in Changsha now, I might say. I have tried it a few times but it's a no go. They all mean something by what they say and eyebrow their dumbbell partners when they don't do what they mean, or should have meant, by what they bid. It's a great life. Almost all the people in business are going away on leave so there will be a new crop along in a few months.

I am to have August 15 to September 15 off and hope to go to Kuling. I don't know anyone I care to go with or stay with yet so shall not make plans until later.

There's a car outside my window just now, the auto of Dr. Yen, our head doctor. It is about the size of your Ford. I can look over the top of it and the passengers sit tandem. It is well-suited for the roads here. I'd like to jump out and take a ride. Speaking of riding, I haven't renewed my efforts in that line yet, though there are four horses indirectly related to our staff. I hope to try myself there soon. I've had the

Kuling Poster

most miserable lumbago for five weeks, old age for sure. I bake under a light every evening in the hospital, somewhat like a Turkish bath.

The Branches have a tennis court in back of their house and we had a regular time yesterday with the officers from the Italian and British gunboats in full colors. They are a great outfit and Mrs. Branch in good Biarritz[32] afternoon tea style was the gracious host. She seems to go in strong for the foreign—that is, the European—style, rather than the bachelors whom she used to collect.

River Gunboat

---

32. A luxurious French seaside town synonymous with high-style fashion.

April 1, 1926 ~ Changsha

Dear Hank,

April fools! I didn't quite finish this the other night. I was interrupted here by the entrance of my pet in the medical school. He is a long, lanky lad named Liu who has the most charming sense of humor. I have had several rounds with him in the hall or the office and ducked yet over some of his miscellaneous cracks. It is a darned shame some really interesting people are, like Dr. Liu, not only Chinese but Interns or Residents, so it hardly does for one in my position to see them socially. For instance, nothing would be more refreshing than to go for a hike or ride with one of them and sit by the fire afterward, as it were, but one must remember to be a good example to the little nurses and respect the country's customs.

Liu told me a good one the other day. He went across the road to get some oranges but they were having the windup of their week's funeral celebrations for grandma. So instead of buying some oranges, he listened to the Tao[33] priest call all the spirits to eat the food prepared for them there. All the people were very quiet and the priest was chanting and calling on the gambler ghosts and those who didn't gamble, the ones with long beards, the ones with no beards, the fat ones, the thin ones, the short ones and the tall ones. At this point, Liu, who had on a dark gown and had come in quietly, spoke from his height of over six foot "Is anyone calling me?" There was great consternation and he departed quickly before he saw the final effect. I can imagine a crazy student at home pulling a stunt like that, but it's hard to think of a Chinese doing it.

I haven't heard from my Irish friend from the boat but can imagine he is busy dashing about Shanghai as well as being a poor correspondent. Mrs. Plumer, who was our guardian angel, reports all is merry there and she's having the time of her life.

As for other little friends, the Dutchman writes he is engaged and the Consul Burke is engaged! The Englishman with the Great Dane dog is on his way home to be engaged!

---

33. Taoism, the basic, eternal principle that the universe transcends reality and is the source of being, non-being, and change.

And, "Here we have reached the summit" has not been heard from at all. How I ask you! I might just as well have stayed at home and contented myself with the dissipations of the church beau.

I'm counting on you to give me lurid details of our dear old Bob's progress. I ought to know everything there, shouldn't I? Also, I'm saving my pennies for our 1927 jag. I think it would be better for you to disembark at Shanghai, or even in Japan on your way over. If travel is good, in the latter case go up through Korea to Peking, then come by rail second-class to Hankou and join me there. It would cost much less than to go to Manila and would give you a real sight of China.

April 5, 1926 ~ Changsha

Dear Mother,

I seem to be literally inclined this evening so shall dash off an epistle to the family before the inclination changes. We all seem to be thriving at present. I have recovered from the lumbago and I think spring has come. We are having lovely balmy days and it is not too hot yet. As to the lumbago, I rather began to doubt whether I would ever get over that. It sure did stick by me, in the absence of static, of course, but I fooled it this time all right.

I feel fine now and ready to take on the whole Chinese army, whatever that is. Speaking of politics, we haven't the slightest idea of what's going on in the great outside world. It may be there is fighting in Hankou or that Peking was burned up last week and we are none the wiser. The answer is, they have cut the telegraph wires from here to Hankou, and the trains can only run from here to Yochow[34], and the river has been so low large steamers cannot run so our mail has been delayed. The result here is everybody is quite calm and happy without having to worry about the fate of our neighbors.

You probably know more about the political situation here in China at this moment than I do myself. At least you may have had more opportunity to read about it in the newspapers. You know by experience it does not mean you thereby know any more. We have martial law in the city so anyone who wants to go through at night has to have

---

34. Presently, Yueyang is a prefecture-level city in the northeast corner of Hunan province on the southern shores of Dongting Lake

the password, and they are very strict about it. My own experience has been that I have returned at night with no sign of a sentry, let alone a person calling for the password.

I do not know how the Governor is panning out, though the general impression is he is with the southern Red element. I don't know what he will do about it. We have had no indication of anti-foreign feeling, except for a parade the other day in protest against the latest student shooting affair in Peking, when there were quite a few students killed by Chinese guards around the President's palace when the students tried to get in there. When they paraded here they did nothing against the foreigners, of course, except to break a few windows as they went by the Episcopal Mission and the YMCA.

I have been negotiating with the proper authorities on the subject of changing my living quarters to the women's dorm next to the hospital. It is not as formidable as it sounds, as there are six women students, I think, and they live in a house about the size of the one I am in now.

Downstairs, Dr. Walters and Dr. Ching have their quarters. The former is going to Peking for six weeks beginning the fourth of May, which means she will leave here next week sometime as she has to go all the way by boat around by Shanghai.

I have not asked Dr. Ching what she thinks of it, but we are good friends and I think would find it quite agreeable. Personally, I would find it more independent than I feel here, and I also think it would be more economical. I am interested in saving the pennies and see no particular reason why I should pay $60 a month when I might live for $45 and enjoy as much social life and more privacy. If I go, it will be for the last half of April and May and June. It would also be more convenient to the hospital.

Yesterday was Easter but I had no chance to go to church at all. I was on duty from 7 to 7, but hoped to be able to go over to part of the service at least. Just at noon, however, they brought in a boy who had been very badly burned in a school fire and we cared for him until he died late in the afternoon. He was fairly roasted, and the skin of his fingers came off like gloves, and about as thick as kid gloves. It was a horrible business and seemed very sad, as he had just come from upriver to go to school here.

They all said our Easter Service was a very fine one, well arranged and a good sermon by Dr. Preston. I had no new hat to wear anyhow and of course that takes some joy out of life. However, I was given an Easter present—the crest of a night heron. The Medical student Liu had shot it himself and then scalped it. The feathers are very fine and of a steel blue color and from the middle grow four long, wispy, sort of sharp-pointed feathers about five or 6 inches long. It would look fine on the side of a felt hat either red or gray, but this is hardly the season for anything like that.

I wrote to Mrs. Hooker in Shanghai and asked her if she would send me a small-brimmed white straw hat of Panama or manila or something of that sort—sort of a sport hat for the summer. She said, in a rash moment, that she would be glad to do any shopping for me, so I shall take her up on it to that extent.

I wrote to Burns today that I was sending him the long-promised kite. I just happened to wonder whether it might be against the law to fly it in the city because of the long string falling across the streets if it should break or something. I suggested they might fly it on the campus. I had not thought of the Byrne neighborhood, though that might he a good place also.

I got it through a man in the Hsiang-Ya Hospital office who is nearly 50 years old, but quite a kite flier. He is also a rare old sport and likes a good time, playing with his friends in the evenings as well as flying kites in the daytime. He made himself one, which is a powerful puller when in the air. I thought it would pull him over the roof's edge, so I urged him to write from Canton when the strong wind took him there and he assured me he would let us know about the weather in Singapore this time of year.

If you have any superfluous newspaper picture copies of your charming daughter, besides the one you are sending her, will you send one on to Clarice?

I have finally paid off the man in Swanton for the linen and now feel it is mine. I have written to Jo to send what is left of it back to you to keep in cold storage for me until I come home or she brings it this summer to Seattle when they come out. If there is any of it you would care to have, please do so. Neither Dwight nor Jo have ever eluded vague responsibility of reimbursing me for what they sold in New Haven, but they may do it someday. I don't feel interested in any further efforts to sell any of it and am satisfied to have such beautiful acquisitions to the family linen.

The family is at the moment at their favorite indoor sport of bridge, which makes me wonder how the cribbage is coming. I hope well and satisfactorily. I want to learn it someday.

April 13, 1926 ~ Changsha

Dear Mother,

This would seem to be Eunice's birthday, which means yesterday was Burns's. And right here I would like to warn him the long-promised kite is still here and I am making another attempt to send it. The box was too large to send by parcel post so I thought I might send it by freight. Unfortunately, there was no company here which could send it through without a break in Shanghai, and I have found out since the minimum freight charge is $10 US. Therefore I shall divide it up still smaller and send it in two or more sections to Seattle by parcel post. I am almost disgusted with it only that I have made up my mind to send it and hate to have to renege.

All the flowers are coming out and we have sweet peas and the locust trees are in bud and I do think spring has come. I suppose it is an old story in Seattle where the things were beginning to bud before I left. I hope there was no freezing weather to ruin the things.

I have been riding a couple of times to see what it would do to my lumbago and found the dread malady has entirely gone. The trail to Chu Garden is lovely this time of year and the Magnolia trees and the Judas bushes and flowering peach and plum were lovely there in the garden. The only trouble is that instead of gum wrappers and cigarette stubs there are peanut shells and watermelon seeds all over the walks out there, and the pond that should by rights reflect the beautiful trees was all covered with green slime and dotted with decaying cabbage leaves. I wish Louise Jordan Milne would see it before she writes another *Shantung Garden*.

The ponies are a bit seedy after a winter's rest, and do not seem at all well. I rode the second day with Les Walker and his nag was so fuzzy he could have had braids made in this coat anywhere. Just the same, the animals do cover the ground, which is the main consideration, and I continue to get as big a thrill from the rice paddy fields and unusual little old houses as I ever did before. I think if I ever get really tired of them I would have no hankering for China again. But, I do find them attractive which contributes a lot to the vista's joys.

Hospital work is a bit heavy just now. Miss Beebe is sick again so I have some of her work along with my own. We are just having a sort of flu epidemic among the medical students. I think they got some bad food on Saturday because since then we have admitted fifteen of them and discharged a couple after only one day's fever. It has meant a lot of shifting of beds and all that but we are all getting along very pleasantly. Fortunately, I seem to stand in well with the interns and residents so we have no quarreling on the wards or difficulties with the doctor side of the game. We have had a few refugees come in, some people who go straggling in and out of the city every day, arriving in trains from goodness knows where, getting their rice and then leaving on the train again. It is a sad sight. I wish I could think of a good story to go with the pictures I have in my head, crowds of them trailing up the road. One dramatic detail is, as they receive their rice they are marked with a blue streak across one cheek. So each, from the largest to the smallest, has this identification on their faces.

Speaking of refugees, the intern Liu picked up one on the road a couple of days ago, a girl of nine, the thinnest thing I have seen for some time. Her face looked like a thin elderly lady's of about 80. After she had been in for a few hours, they discovered she was just recovering from smallpox, so we vaccinated everyone else on the ward. She survived until this morning when she passed 46 worms at one time and then died. Goodness knows how many more animals she may have had in her interior. I presume they will do an autopsy.

I am moving this weekend to the dormitory, which was built two years ago for women students. Dr. Walters who has the X-ray and Dr. Ching, in charge of Obstetrics, occupy the front half of the building at present. It consists of a living-dining room downstairs and two bedrooms each with a berth, and a sleeping porch upstairs. I shall use the sleeping porch and one student's room, which is now empty. Dr.

Walters will go to Peking next week for a course in X-ray, after which I shall occupy her room. Each bedroom has a stove like the one in your sitting room that is the best heating arrangement for a room, which is not occupied from morning till night. I think it will be quite a cheerful arrangement, affording variety, privacy and economy. I ought to be able to live there for $40–$45 a month, whereas it is $60 where I am now.

To be sure the Branches put on more style and have teas and musicals and all, which is fine, but which I do not care to pay for.

The intern Liu, with whom I made a bargain before I went home in '24 to supply cigarettes or tobacco in exchange for pheasant feathers, has come through with 92 perfectly beautiful feathers. My original intention was to have them made into a fan like the peacock feather fans, but there are more in this collection than I need for that. I shall guard them tenderly as he says they represent the expenditure of 500 pounds of sweat and 500 dollars worth of cartridges and have taken five years to collect and are for exchange only. I have asked Dwight to supply the tobacco. I hope he doesn't forget it or I shall lose much face.

There are many parties in the wind these days, saying good-bye to people who are leaving. I see they are still up to it just as before, either welcoming or farewell-ing different ones. I can't work up any deep regret at seeing any of them depart and find greater satisfaction in the hope their successors may be an improvement. I enjoy the affairs, but suspect my enthusiasm may not be keen, because I don't happen to be in love with any of them and none of them are madly pursuing me. I believe it probably makes a difference in one's zest.

I have no more literary efforts to offer for publication, but hope to work up to it again one of these days. Apparently it does no harm to attempt sending stories and merely means expenditure of labor and postage stamps with the hope sometime something may be considered worth publishing.

I am wondering if Austin is on the scene yet. I have not heard from him at all, but seem to remember this was about the time scheduled. I hope all goes well.

April 23, 1926 ~ Changsha

Dear Mother,

It is now about 10:15 p.m. and I have just been to a movie of Wesley Barry's in *School Days*. I think the film is not so painfully old so it was not as bad as *Her Hidden Past*, which I saw here before. The light is never quite strong enough but otherwise it was fine—being a "good clean play" and all that. At the present I am writing on a board on my lap in the operating room watching a patient who is having diathermy. He is half my practice, as it were, the other being the woman with the infected hands. I am glad to say she is improving rapidly now, but how much of her improvement is due to the ten incisions she has from her elbow down and how much to diathermy I don't know. She certainly had a terrible-looking mess for a while. The boy has an infected elbow that is improving. I have not used the treatment on any medical cases or on any other patients at all, chiefly because no doctors are familiar with the technique and because we have no proper electrodes. The ones I am using are made of old standard oil tins. They do well enough as conductors but are no good for fitting the figure. We are experimenting with other metals from the street. They cannot get the pewter thin enough as it is pounded by hand. Dr. Kiang, Peter's brother, thinks he can get something suitable. He is to be understudy apparently, as he seems to be more interested and is mechanically inclined.

He is the one who was nearly cut in two or carried away by the huge kite he was flying from the hospital roof last week. The pull was very strong and he tied the cord around his waist and insisted upon doing it alone. I had visions of him sailing off to Canton. He is a fine-looking chap and quite clever. He has been here long enough to be getting it so will go away next year to Peking, I think.

We are having very mild weather here and a lack of accustomed rain. The farmers are quite in despair after one year of flooding in 1924 followed by a year of drought last year. We feel the effects of numbers of refugees who still come and go. Rice has increased in price from $8 per some weight to $15 for the same amount. This is time to plant rice and though there is enough water to start there is not enough to last for the floode ields.

Xiang River Flood Damage

The Buddhists declared a boycott against killing meat, fish or using eggs, so we've been vegetarians for the past few days. It is in the nature of a fast to please the Deity, though I have heard the Rain God doesn't like to hear the squeal of pigs being slaughtered. As the present boycott seems to include other animals as well as pigs, the theory is not altogether sound.

I am living with Drs. Walters and Ching at present. The latter, a Chinese, as you see. It would sound scandalous were it not they are both women and quite calm and businesslike. They have the front half of the women's dormitory for the coeds next to the hospital. They have a large living-dining room across the front with a porch on the East. Upstairs each has a bedroom and bath with a sleeping porch for both. I live in a vacant coed's rooms and share Ota Walters' bathroom. She expects to go to Peking next week so I will take her bedroom then.

My room has some rather giddy red furniture consisting of a couple of tables with drawers and a chiffonier. I bought some cloth like the blue and white Chinese bedspread and made curtains for the window and the closet-shelf affair in the corner. With a piece of matting intended for a bed on the floor, I am quite cozy. None of us are home during the day so we do not feel at all crowded, and it is about half as costly as living with the Branches. We have Chinese food every noon and I seem to thrive on it. Sarah Ching is from the University of Pennsylvania and talks quite scathingly at times about "these Chinese," yet she has adapted herself quite successfully and enjoys her work.

Dr. Sarah Ching

Les Walker and I had a lovely hike up Yolo-san last week starting about 5 p.m. We went a new way which led us out at the South end. We hiked quite lustily until 8 o'clock and were then at the very summit from which we could see in all directions by moonlight. It was lovely and there we perched among the bats and bugs—or other bats and bugs, I should say, and had our picnic supper.

He is a very attractive youth and I find him most congenial. He is the one who was Clarice's special pal last year, so we have something as a common interest besides general taste. Coming home we took a sampan across the river urging him up to the north end of the "range" and brought us as far as the Yali Road, which he declined to take because there were passengers calling him from the other side. So we rode over to pick up the passengers, re-cross and then come down the river. The others proved to be eight coolies carrying a coffin and the gentleman whose relative's remains were within—cheerful company for a rowboat, particularly at 12 midnight. Talk about Charon and the Styx! Eventually we did float home, after which I was so cruel as to drag the two diathermy patients from their slumbers for treatments.

The heater arrived safe and I just changed the plug to fit our house, but we haven't used it yet. It's a nice heater. I sent the kite back in the same case and I think there are some $1 postage stamps on the inner cover if Dad wants them for Burns's album. I wish I could convert the heater into a fan when necessary, though I shall certainly appreciate it as is next year.

Am glad to hear good news of you all. When do the Eunices[35] go east? I hope they miss measles or the itch or whatever it is still due them.

April 27, 1926 ~ Changsha

Dear Mother,

I have just met Father's friend, Mr. Shaw, in the hospital hall. He seems to have been paging me for some time but I had not run into him before. He seems to be feeling quite well, though he has the same sort of ascetic expression on his face and I keep wondering whether he would whip out a long list of symptoms and maladies to which his feeble flesh seems heir.

He asked to be remembered to Father and spoke of how kind Harold Smith had been to him. I asked him what he is doing now and it seems to be the same as he was doing before he left America—namely nothing. He said when he first came back he found his wife was sick so he had to go to his home some distance from here for a while, but she apparently recovered enough to allow him to return here. He said some of his friends want him to teach somewhere but he is not sure whether he will or not. I should not think the present time of year would offer very good opportunities for starting teaching. I wonder how much he is traveling on the face of having been studying in the great USA. He is a rare bird. I told him to come over to tea someday and as he is still hanging around, I rather suspect he is going to make it this day. Fortunately, it has been raining the past two days so I hope the farmers have taken a bit of hope to begin to plant their rice in earnest.

Sunday I went for quite a long walk with Ota Walters. We started at 11 o'clock in the morning and walked until 2. We crossed over the river just north of here and wandered along the riverbank and along the far side until it comes to a sharp bend in the river where there is a ferry. There we crossed back again and we arrived home very hungry for late tiffin.

---

35. The Eunices refers to her sister Eunice and her husband Harry.

On the far side, we could see over the farms where they should now be planting rice. Most fields were dry, though a few of them were covered with water. Apparently it takes a good lusty soaking to properly prepare the soil for the rice. In many places they had all their forces at work getting the river water up over the banks into the fields. On the river's edge there would be a paddlewheel arrangement with three or four

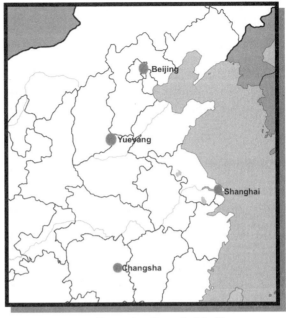

Yueyang:Changsha:Shanghai:Beijing

people sitting on the crossbar, working the paddles with their feet. That would keep in motion a sort of continuous chain of paddles that forced the water uphill to a sort of pool part way up the bank. There would be a water buffalo harnessed to an arrangement like a cogwheel lying on its side, and this wheel would in turn keep another endless chain of paddles in motion to force the water up the rest of the way.

Primitive? I should say so, but very picturesque. Unfortunately, it is not so efficient as it is interesting and quaint. I couldn't but wonder what they would do with a donkey engine and a real life-sized hose that would take more water up in an hour than they could get up in a day. I also wondered to myself why one of the hundreds of students who are educated in foreign countries do not turn their attention to the problems of famine in these districts; to the need for a bit of irrigation and the turning aside of some of the main streams flooding the parts needing irrigation at the times when they need water.

I suppose it is because they belong to the student class and must do big things like directing the engineering of something where they get lots of face and plenty of squeeze or teaching where there they are really gentlemen and do not identify themselves with the poor farmers. It does seem a distraction of talent and energy.

After returning from the long walk which was about ten miles, I had a note from Les Walker asking me to go riding, so after a short snooze I went with him out the wide military road toward Siangtan. I don't know how far we went but it was great fun and a good evening.

At sunset we sat on a gravestone and surveyed the countryside, which was largely occupied in our immediate vicinity by a poor woman and her four children. She looked quite ill as she insisted she was, and I was sorry I did not have some money with me to give to her. The next youngest picked up a cigarette stub which Les had dropped on the ground and tried to smoke it wrong end, which was funnier to us than it was to him. Very precocious child. There are many beggars and refugees still around here.

They seem to be having some kind of war somewhere between here and Yueyang, though I don't know just where nor how serious it is. It is between our present Governor Tan and the Hunan Division of General Wu P`ei-fu's troops. The latter is not popular here at all it seems, and even the students in the city last week had a meeting and decided if he sent his troops here to Changsha they would take up arms themselves. Some say it would not be a bad idea, and nothing would cure the students of their military tendencies so well as having to pack a gun around for a while. It would be a sad state of affairs if it should happen.

They are a hotheaded outfit certainly, and on parade have little use for the Yale students who do not go out with them every time they have one to honor some Peking students or others. I wish their energies too might be directed to some good, constructive cause.

We have two wounded officers in the hospital now. One has lacerated wounds over his head inflicted by his own soldiers who tried to revolt against him. He is a fat, uninteresting-looking sort of bloke and I cannot blame his soldiers very much if he acts as he looks. The other is one who was shot in the leg at the fighting below here last Saturday. He seems like a fine fellow with a history of TB and a rather delicate sort of person. He was shot through the thigh and has had an infection starting up, and an anything but cheerful prospect ahead of him.

You probably have later news than I have about what is happening in other parts of China, though it may not be very accurate. We have no telegraph connections to Hankou or to any other city, of course, as all our telegrams come through Hankou, and the trains are held up as the past few days' fighting has disturbed traffic. Therefore, all our mail comes up by boat once or twice a week and is necessarily somewhat out-of-date.

Locally, everything is so peaceful it is hard to believe there is anything like trouble near or far away. It is inconvenient as many people are trying to make plans for the summer. It looks as though no one would go north to Peitaho province or Peking without going by water by way of Shanghai, which is a very long and expensive trip.

My patient with the infected hand has been discharged to return for daily dressings and the boy with the bad elbow is better locally, but seems to have some generalized infection due perhaps to a very badly infected and crusted scalp. So many youngsters have scabby heads and it is particularly bad in the warm weather when the flies crawl all over.

Dr. Houston submitted to one treatment for a rheumatic wrist. (Though Dr. Clarence Smith says there is no such thing as rheumatism!) I suspect he is gout-ish as they live very well and very high at their house and imbibe occasionally. He is getting quite fat as an evidence of high living. He said it felt all right afterward but he was quite low the next day and vowed he would never let me do it again. That doesn't make me mad at all as it took a great deal of my off-time duty to attend to diathermy patients as the electric current doesn't come on until 5:50 p.m. these days and is on for about 12 hours.

I just received in the mail a receipt for the linen bill I had paid. I discounted it 5% and they made no comment so the linen is now mine and I think I'll consider what is left as my personal property with no particular effort to see any more of it.

May will soon be here with its over quota of holidays. I think the students celebrate four humiliation days to commemorate various times when students have been killed in protesting against something somewhere. May 30th will be the main blowout, I suppose.

The Medical School has just been given $80,000 indemnity money and as much more from other sources toward their goal of $250.000. It really looks now as though we were on a better basis than the college side. We are supposed to be entirely under Chinese supervision and all is merry. Sarah Ching says she is afraid they will replace foreigners with Chinese-trained until the standard will drop. She practically considers herself a foreigner and speaks quite scathingly of "these Chinese."

Young Hospital Patients

I hope you are all quite well and enjoying good weather and the apartments across the street. That will make a great change in neighborhood appearance certainly. Did they leave the lot on Fourteenth Avenue vacant?

May 4, 1926 ~ Changsha

To Elizabeth Henry aka Hank

Some time has elapsed since last I penned an epistle to you, but not very much of interest has occurred in the meantime. Still, there might be enough to tell the folks at home about.

Politically we have had a really amusing time. Fortunately, it has not been more than that for us, not even an inconvenience. About six weeks ago, the man who was our Governor for several years, a man named, Zhao Heng-Ti[36], departed with all his advisors to Yochow,[37]

36. ZHAO HENG-TI, born in Hunan Province, 1880; graduated from the Japanese Military Cadets' College in Tokyo, Japan, there, specializing in artillery; during the 1911 Revolution, he joined Kuomintang party and was appointed commander of a revolutionary army in Hunan. Zhao Heng-ti, the ruler of Hunan (1926), was an agent of the Northern warlords when the Northern Expeditionary Army overthrew.

37. Yueyang is a prefecture-level city at the northeastern corner of Hunan province.

and then to Hankou. We never knew just why he left when he did, but suspect it may have had something to do with a certain Tang Sen Chi upriver who, incidentally, was threatening to slap his wrist and kick him out of office.

As it is under such circumstances, the threatened one prefers to clear out, grabbing all spare cash and rolls of silk and whatnot, appoint his enemy his successor in polite language, and thereby save a great deal of discomfort, expense, loss of life and not to mention, face.

Lately, Gov. Tang's men have gone Yochow-ward to thumb their noses at ex-Governor Chao's friends, particularly one Yeh K'ai Shing[38] (Ye Ting), a former member of Chao's army and now a henchman of his majesty General Wu P'ei-fu. All reports we heard were to the effect Tang's army was gradually shoving General Ye Ting's army out of the province of Hunan. As General Ye Ting is a friend of Canton and though not actually Red is decidedly pinkish, the students swore allegiance to him, published a newspaper against General Wu P'ei-fu, and put up posters throughout the city depicting General Ye Ting eating the flesh of "Hunan"!

The more radical students in the city went so far as to hold a meeting and resolve to take arms against General Wu if necessary to keep him out of the province. I'm afraid some foreigners almost hoped they would, much as anyone would hate to see young students sniped. Then we heard General Wu P'ei-fu, through General Ye Ting, had issued a warning: if Hunan avoids alliance with the "2 Kwangs," that is Klang-si and Kwangtung (Canton), he wouldn't come into this province.

That didn't seem to hold somehow, as next we knew Tang had collected all his many trains as possible and beat it south about 40 miles where he is permanently parked. Some of our people were near the railroad the next night when General Ye Ting's men came in on the train and our Professor of history wished to linger and watch history "being made." His wife was much more interested in getting home so started on ahead. Suddenly there was a random shot from somewhere

---

38. Ye Ting, joined the Kuomintang when Sun Yat-sen founded it in 1919 (originally known as the Chinese Revolutionary Party). By 1921 he was a battalion commander in the National Revolutionary Army. In 1926 he led an advanced detachment during the Northern Expedition, ultimately achieving several victories, including the September besiegement of Wuchang, breaking through the defenses on the 10th of October.

into the air and he decided he'd seen quite enough history himself.

Tomorrow, General Ye Ting himself will come and be the Governor putting us in a class of well-organized provinces again. Two battleships, if one can call them such, came in yesterday afternoon, so we look quite military though we may not act so. The students have reacted in quite a typical way. When they heard Tang had gone, many ardent speechmakers departed also. Much better to resign than wait to be fired.

A group of men and women students had gone to where Tang's army was fighting last week, the former to encourage the soldiers and the latter to be Red Cross nurses. The soldiers let them know they didn't care to be encouraged by any

General Ye Ting
(Wikipedia)

crazy students and the girls found they didn't know anything about nursing after all, so they returned chastened and chastised.

Speaking of chastising, the favorite outdoor sport of newly arrived soldiery is to stop students on the street, ask if they are students, and then punch them a bit and treat them rough in a mild way. Two of our fiercest young agitators came home weeping, more because of outraged feelings than from bodily injuries. We cannot help but feel a certain satisfaction in seeing them get

Kwangsi Troops Drilling

the spankings they deserve and which some of us have been aching to give them. When received from their own people, from the province too, they cannot blame foreigners.

So I am now living with two unmarried doctors, one a Chinese. Sounds bad, doesn't it. However, both are women and a bit older than I. The Chinese one is a peach and very clever, from Pennsylvania. The other is a gloomy kind of customer, no pep, suffering disillusionment in her third year here. She wouldn't be so bad if she gave herself half a chance. She departs for Peking this Saturday, so Sarah Ching and I will reign together. We live in the front half of the women's dormitory. There are six women students in Yale-in-China, unnecessary adjuncts I would say, but as they are here it seems necessary to house them.

Mrs. Walters is their Dean and when she goes they come under my tender care. I shall have to change if I'm to set them a good example. The Chinese nurses are moving into a new house about the equivalent of two blocks from here. It is just being finished and is the property of a General Li Chong[39]. He is unfortunately out of favor with the powers that be, so has fled leaving his younger brother to finish supervising the finishing touches. The brother came over here to beg Dr. Yen to occupy it or send some hospital staff there, as he is afraid some soldiers will take it over. His fears are well-founded, as this is just what a general or his army would love to do.

I shall move there the middle of June and stay until the middle of August when I go vacationing. It will give me a fine opportunity to gather more Chinese language. Even so, I shall not assume the task of writing poetry like my friend Jane. It is hard enough to translate plain prose, let along the interpretation of the soul and meaning of poetry. This may be my fourth year in China but I don't know enough yet for that.

As for high society, it isn't very high at present; not so many parties as formerly. However, I did attend one at the Commissioner of Customs. He is a Frenchman and had invited all the foreigners in port, as well as the Chinese doctor and family from here. It was quite giddy. We all danced and imbibed a bit of champagne.

There have been one or two lesser affairs but the "younger set" has been so largely superseded by older married couples that it's not quite

---

39. General Li Chong was the last Protector General of the Western Regions

so lively as before. Now this is confidential, merely for the luncheon duo: I've picked me up one of the bachelors for a little playmate. He's the one who acted in a similar role for my friend Clarice Lewis last year, so I guess he's used to it. Anyhow, I have had such a time trying to find a congenial soul, he fitted in nicely. We've been riding and hiking and a bit of dancing, but the darnedest part of it is, it is exceedingly difficult to maintain it on such a basis. After all, spring comes but once a year and in another month or so he will have departed and I'll probably never see him again. That's the way of the East, but it's somewhat wearing. I'm not contemplating annexing him permanently and neither is he; we shall bumble along merrily and hope to survive. When the river clears we are going to add swimming to our list of diversions, which will help in hot weather. At present we cool off by going to the river and hanging our feet off into space and watching the shooting stars. It's a bit dangerous but very pleasant, so that's that.

Any hope on the transPacific trip for '27?

May 9, 1926 ~ Changsha

Dear Mother,

I received one letter from you yesterday enclosing the communication from the Holyoke people and referring to the letter you said you had written the day before. I am still waiting for that one and hope it will come today. They say the trains are running again with other cargo than soldiers so we may begin to have mail again every day rather than twice a week when the boats come in.

Speaking of boats, the latest additions to our fleet in the river are three of Wu P'ei-fu's gunboats. I have not seen them at close enough range to know just what sort of things they are but if they are the same ones I saw at Swatow three years ago, they may be all right on looks but were reported then to be able to make about six knots. At that speed, I guess they are so much speedier than any other river craft, except for passenger and foreign vessels, that they could chase a whole fleet of junks and overtake them. That is, providing the wind and current were not with the junks. The political situation is really very interesting these days, and as long as they continue their bloodless warfare, quite harmless to the ordinary citizen. We have not had a Governor for about a week now and it is daily reported General Ye Ting will come in. He is one of Wu P`ei-fu's men and an old friend and soldier of our former governor Chan Heng-ti.

When Chao left over a month ago he appointed as his successor the man Tang Sen Chi from upriver who was threatening to come down here and show Chao what was what and slap his wrist and kick him out. By Chao's appointing him his successor, and having the provincial assembly approve the appointment, there was nothing left to do here but shoot off many firecrackers and then execute a few dangerous political men. Rather hard on them, but an easy way out of it for the common rabble.

Tang was only able to stick it out for about six weeks. He has gone downriver to the north of the province to Yechow and was there doing battle with friend General Ye Ting. The latter being backed by Wu, it was hard for an upstart like Tang to get very far and though we kept hearing how successful Tang was, it was not long before his soldiers all came running back again. It was while the reports of his victory were in the air the students got together and decided they would oppose Wu P`ei-fu even to the extent of taking up arms against him. They even published an anti-Wu paper, but it died a quick death and the students who made the loudest noise developed sick grandmothers in Hankou and beat it off on the boat.

Some of our people were out for dinner the night the troops of Tang left, and they said it was quite a sight. Reverend Hail, particularly, who is interested in history, wanted to stand on the bank above the tracks and watch history in the making, but his wife was more interested in getting home, Rev. Hail says. Quite soon after someone let off a firecracker, it reminded him he ought to catch up to his wife, so he really had to run to catch her. Her version is not quite the same as she says it was a gun and he nearly ran past her.

There are many soldiers in the city but they seem quite well-behaved, though some of them are dangerously armed. The first two days they were here they had a playful way of accosting students and then spanking them either with the flat of their swords or with their hands. Of course, it was not necessary to hit them hard to outrage their dignity, and send some of them home in tears. Cruel it may seem but some foreigners were quite pleased at the chastising as they had longed to do it themselves many times. I understand since then the soldiers have been instructed not to lay hands on any students and if they do they will be beheaded, which is stern enough.

To be sure, the threats and fulfillments on the beheading business are not very kind and seem a bit savage but I can't help but think it would not be a bad idea to introduce it into some of our civilized countries. I really think it might help to check some crime. Certainly there is a reasonably low rate of crime in this city, if one can judge by observation and hearsay. Being unable to read the papers, I can't judge from them, but whenever I ask anyone about news in the paper it is usually about some military operations or about some fair or exhibition or something similar.

Dr. Yen and Mr. Tsao (Hospital Manager) have been entertaining many guests the last two weeks, some of them rather unexpected,. The answer being, when the situation becomes a bit thick, these political gentlemen from the city come dashing out here to see their friends until everything clears up again. We had three of them in the hospital. One had the diagnosis "for observation," one of "diarrhea," and the third —who must have been less popular—"malingering." I guess the latter diagnosis would have fitted any of them. The second one is the principal at a very radical and Red school in the city and General Ye Ting's men were after him. Two heavily armed soldiers came to the hospital the other morning and asked for him but the door coolie said he was not here. In fact, he had not come to the ward yet, though his chart was there, for he was hiding in the office of Mr. Tsao. Later in the afternoon, he went to the room and then they did a gastric analysis on him that was good punishment I would say.

Ota Walters, with whom I have been living the last few weeks, has just gone to Peking for some study in X-ray. She will be gone about 2 months and it leaves Sarah Ching and I alone for the time being. Before Ota gets back, Sarah will have left. The spring exodus has begun. I enjoy Sarah very much.

She is a very bright young woman and doesn't put up with any funny business from "these Chinese," as she calls them. The sad part is she seems to have developed some pulmonary trouble and will go to America in another month. She is not particularly surprised, as she has had significant bronchial trouble since she has been here and has had pneumonia once. She is due to leave now anyhow, but it is too bad her health is not good. She is a very husky person, weighs about 160, and has good color, but is deceiving like so many TB people.

She will go to San Francisco or rather Berkeley where her foster parents live—people named Nash. She then expects to go to Yosemite somewhere and rest. She knows Dr. Force, having studied with him at the University of California where she graduated in '17.

After she goes, I shall move over with the Chinese nurses. They have just been transferred from the hospital's third floor where they have been for four years into a brand-new house about 2 blocks distant from here. The new house was built by a man named Chong, the first of our refugee political patients, and is just now being furnished. There are about eleven very large rooms, rather peculiarly arranged, and 17 servants' rooms. The nurses are in the main house and in 10 servants' rooms on the upper floor. There is running water and regular bathrooms, which are quite elegant, and it is well screened throughout, even having screen doors between the rooms. The nurses were a bit peeved because they say it is too far to walk, particularly in wet weather, which is true, but its advantages so far outweigh that they were reconciled. There is quite a large garden and cool fresh air that they will appreciate in the summer time. I shall go there the middle of June and stay until I go on my vacation in the middle of August. I hope to have a Chinese teacher for those months and with the nurses to practice on, really learn a little Chinese. I should like to know enough to be able to read.

Friday was a holiday, supposedly, being Humiliation Day for some Japanese insult. The city students were planning to parade and make their usual demonstrations, but the city was put under martial law and the students advised to keep off the streets. We are hoping the same will be in effect on May 30. It is hard to believe a year ago there was anti-foreign feeling for we certainly get none of it now. They may revive some of it on the 30th for my benefit.

I was interested to hear Mrs. Hail say she had heard from Katherine the Blacks were not coming here for the present after all. I thought only Mrs. Black was coming, but it seems Antoinette was planning to come too and teach in the Bible Institute if it pleased her. They asked the advice of a businessperson in Shanghai and he told them he would not advise their coming right now.

I might say I am afraid they will wait a long time before they get the encouragement of a Shanghai person, as they are gloomy over the foreigners' situation in China anyhow and they are all convinced Changsha is a terrible place, off in the wilds and full of bandits and no decent place for a decent person to go. That was the opinion expressed to me by some Shanghai men on the ship coming over, but they think anything further away than Woosung[40] is wild. I shall be interested to know if they really do come. They might ask E.L.'s advice, in which case they would stay home for a long time, I think.

Now is the proper time to order some Peking rugs if you or any others in the family want any. Ota will get them in Peking and bring them down with her when she comes in July. I can keep them until I go home next summer.

Will you find out if any want rugs; if so, sizes and colors, preferably by a sample of cloth or paper. I am going on the assumption they will be about $1.50 per square foot, Mex. of course. Please do not send the money as I have enough in the bank to pay for several and exchange is unfavorable for buying gold, as I shall have to do a bit later to pay insurance. I hope to be able to have Ota buy a small one or so for me, but shall be glad to do my part of getting any more for you. If you can find out rather soon and let me know, we shall have time to get all the ordering, etc., done. While on the subject, if anyone wants brass or copper or pewter things made, will you let me know? I have a man who does cross-stitching so I hope to have as much of that as I want done at home.

I continue to ride once or twice a week, usually with Les Walker. He is a fine person, agreeable as Sandy used to be, but with more pep and a size or so larger. The horses have been sort of sick so do not have their former spunk, yet they do cover the ground rapidly so one does not have to go far to be out of civilization. About 10 minutes' walk takes one into the country.

The bachelors went off on a junk trip this weekend, Friday being a holiday, so they have been gone since Thursday, the lucky dogs. I

40. Woosung was a port town located downriver from Shanghai

do not know when they will return but imagine it will be tomorrow morning, about 10 minutes before they have to appear in class. That is what I should do, I am sure.

I have been wondering for about a month now about the heir to the Austin Smith millions. If I remember, he was due to arrive in April sometime, and this being May, something has probably occurred.

I had a letter from the Secretary of the Senior Department, writing to absent members. I suppose. We have not lettered the Pilgrim bed, but they are using the money for a free bed just the same. I think I shall pick out an interesting patient and take it for granted he or she is in the bed and tell them about it.

May 18, 1926 ~ Changsha

Dear Mother,

How do you like the elegant stationery? Earned by me as the back half of a wheelbarrow at a party last Saturday. The affair was held at the home of some new people—the Feelys—and was quite a jolly party. We all had a buffet supper form of feeding that seems to be replacing the more formal kind. It is possible to share more guests when the food is less elaborate and when half of them stand up and eat off the buffet. We played games of carrying peanuts on a knife, and such merriment, beside dancing and cards for those who preferred it.

We had been in the afternoon to a lovely sort of garden party at Mr. Pichon's. He is the Customs Commissioner and lives in the Customs House, which has a beautiful garden around it. There were pomegranate trees in bloom and all sorts of flowers. There is a wall on the South covered with ivy and over the wall on the riverside we could see the junk sails passing, just to remind me we were in China and not in England or America. Hilda Yen was one of the hosts along with Peggy Moore, who would be classified as a quadroon[41] at home only she's quarter Chinese rather than colored.

Hilda is a beautiful girl and wears the most attractive Chinese clothes imaginable, quite distinct from any of the other Chinese girls here. The Customs garden is large enough that 2 tennis courts were laid out there, and on the rest of the green we played games, carrying

41. Quadroon, an offensive term for one with a black and three white grandparents.

eggs in a spoon, threading needles, a four-legged race with 2 men and a girl in each team, and a wheelbarrow race that Les Walker and I won.

After games they all played tennis until dark. We had fresh, wonderful strawberries, but no cream to go with them. Hilda is a charming host but the poor girl is having a thin time here. She enjoys a good time and is so very attractive but all her outside frivolities with us are contrary to her parents' wishes. She was to have gone with her uncle W.W. Yen to England this year, at least that was the premise that brought her here to prepare a wardrobe, but he is to be Premier now but no one knows for how long. She has the prospect of a summer here or in Shanghai with family on all sides of her.

Dr. Yen seems so westernized in many ways, yet he does clamp down the lid on his westernized daughter. She, though educated abroad, is after all a Chinese girl and must obey her parents and do nothing without their consent. Occasionally, she does go against their wishes and always has the feeling she is committing some sin. I wonder what will become of her, and so does she. Not much if she stays in this place with no congenial Chinese to amuse her. She would like to go to Peking again to be with W. W. Yen or to America. Maybe she will go again. She should marry some modern Chinese man of good family and education to keep her happy. Otherwise, foreign men as well as Chinese, are always falling in love with her and making things very difficult.

The Mission very kindly celebrated my birthday last evening by having the annual Mission dinner. It was not a very exciting affair, but everyone seemed pleased and amused. It is the custom for the speakers to slam various members as violently as possible and for the entertainers to do likewise. This year, however, everything was much milder. We were to give a Minstrel Show, but at the last minute they decided not to black up so we just gave the show as we were. Someone had made up some rather good parodies on "Sleep Kentucky Babe"; the "Doctors that Work in the Spring," apropos of the physical exams that have just taken place; "The Missionary Blues," like "Alexander's Ragtime Band." Charlie Keller was the leading light for most of the jokes. He has become so much more middle-aged looking, but is quite a kid in many ways.

Charlie has such a heavy schedule of dates in the cities with all sorts of Chinese committees and has so many of the students and others coming and going in his house, we almost never see him at all. He has thrown himself as strenuously into the Chinese work as he used to concentrate on one thing after another in college, or as seriously as he used to fall in love. He seems much more mature and steadier than before, from what little I've seen of him, and the students are most enthusiastic over him. I haven't asked him if he is anticipating making Yali[42] his permanent residence. It would seem logical for him to stay in China now that he has interest in and knowledge of the country. I heard from someone that he had thought of going into YMCA work, which I should imagine, might be possible.

Speaking of the YMCA, we attended a dinner at the new YMCA building here last week. It is not quite completed but nearly so. The really formal opening will be next fall. The building is modern in every way as far as I can tell, adapted to Chinese use. The reading tables, bowling tables, and Ping-Pong tables are all of beautifully stained camphor wood that would be quite priceless at home. I hate to think of Chinese misusing them, but at least they do not carry pocket knives to carve their names in the desks or tables in time-honored style.

The gym is a fine room and there is a 20-meter long swimming pool. That ought to be fun if the little yellow brothers can refrain from their national pastime of expectorating. Mr. Kiaer, one of the secretaries, assures me it will be very clean, and quite safe for the women to go once a week on Thursday p.m. He wants me to help with instructing the girls to swim. I don't know just what it will come to. I imagine it will be like pulling teeth to get any of the peer bashful creatures into bathing suits and then to enter the water!

Sarah Ching, with whom I live, spends most of her time in bed now. She has chest symptoms and a p.m. temperature, making the doctors suspicious to the extent of making her rest. It seems queer not to have her tearing around, as she is normally a very energetic person. She has not decided where she will go, but is leaving the middle of June, probably for America.

---

42. Yali was founded in 1906 by Yale-in-China, now known as the Yale-China Association. Yali School has a reputation throughout China for quality instruction, as an American-sponsored private school during the first half of the 20th century and as a public school following the 1949 revolution.

Another one, Margaret Muir, will go next week. She was Dr. Hume's secretary for 24-5 but has been sick now for about a year with TB peritonitis. She is strong enough at present to take the trip home. Like most of our victims, she is quite healthy and husky looking; however, a bad expense to the mission.

One of the nurses, Nell Beeby, has not been well since last fall, and they finally decided she has amoebic dysentery so have been giving her emetine. Now she has developed emetine neuritis. What a thought. She varies from 6-hour duty to rest in bed. She will have vacation during July and August and if not perfectly well in September will be sent back to America.

We certainly have terrible luck with single women, making me believe I am of some use to them by just being healthy and on the job. Nearly everyone has had the usual spring cold in more or less severe doses, but except for my lumbago I had when I first came, I have never felt better. I'm hoping it will continue.

I had letters from the aunts last week and from you and Jo. I conclude all is going well at home. I wonder if Jan and Uncle Sam were held up by the strike in England at all. Our British friends have seemed disturbed over the situation, though they are convinced Britain will survive because she always has. It's hard to keep up with the news and I usually depend on Sarah's *N.Y. Times* for months-old news.

Politics here are quite calm again. We seem to get along very well with no Governor in office. The man, Tang Sen Chi, who was put out about 2 weeks ago, is camping somewhere south of the province with the Governor's seals and all, so he is still officially in office, he says. The city is so well organized into the guilds that the wheels turn as usual, Governor or no Governor.

I received the electric stove, many thanks; only it is 110 volt instead of 220, so is of no use to me without a transformer I do not have. That's rather sad, but I've written to Mr. H.H. Braun, the man who was a friend of Helen Hill and is in charge of Anderson-Meyer in Hankou. They handle hardware and electric goods, so I've asked him if I can make an exchange through his company, saving time and postage.

My chief companion in crime these days is Les Walker, one of the bachelors who was a particular friend of Clarice's and for whom

I bought the Victrola records. He is a congenial soul and we manage to ride occasionally or walk now and then. Sunday, he appeared with a lovely little ivory box about the size of a half dollar, but deep; just a little present with the remark of "Happy Birthday." I asked him how he knew it was my birthday and it seems he just said it to be humorous, so the next time he had in tow a gold and black brocade compact case with beautiful ivory beads and tassels, and is the real birthday present. I was quite overcome.

May 27, 1926 ~ Changsha

Dear Hank,

Thank you ever so much for *Gentlemen Prefer Blondes*. I have read about it in book reviews but had not seen a copy. I read some of it to myself and some aloud to my latest boyfriend. We've done quite a bit of reading of one kind or another and Sunday we expect to wander far afield and then lie on our backs under a tree and read some more. I asked if we should go early and come back late. He says he prefers going late and coming back early. Fine idea!

I'll give you a little confidential advice: Don't overdo the matter of "letting down reserve," as our wicked married friend Mrs. Anderson would say. Perhaps a little is O.K. enough so you enjoy dashing here and there together and can appreciate the moon from an esthetic standpoint, but having, in the latest instance, developed it a bit farther, I am in danger of wearying somewhat. It's a bit too strenuous.

Nevertheless, it is exciting and the good old mission would quiver were they to know all the goings-on. Just between you and me, I'll give you an example of how crazy this place makes me. Last Saturday, I went to a party on the island given by the Standard Oil manager. They have a beautiful garden and there were lanterns all over the place, competing with the moon.

About 50 people were present and we had a delicious chicken à la king buffet supper, continued by some delicious loganberry, etc., cocktails. After supper we danced, played cards or mahjong as the spirit moved, or just sat and meditated. The evening became rather hilarious ending with "Farmer in the Dell" and "London Bridge."

Two of the bachelors and I were the only ones from Yali, so after being landed on this side, we tried to get a boat to bring us to our own steps. After a bling down the bund[43] yelling lustily for a sampan, we finally got one and drifted cozily to our own street. By the time we got home it was about 2 a.m., I think. We sat on my porch trying to think of what to do next, so I suggested we go swimming, back in the river where we came from. The bachelors were cheery enough to think it great so Art went over to his house for his suit. I put mine on and gave Les another.

I thought it was a wonderful idea, but just as I was ready to go, Les said he was afraid the gate man would report it to headquarters, as we couldn't possibly be back before about 5:50. Art waited at his house for us and then went to bed, remarking later he never knew Les to be so sober a drunk that he thought of discretion. The result was that Les and I sat on the porch until after 4 in a coil of bathing suits, counting the stars, and being much more scandalous I maintain as he had to pass said gate man going back to his rooms. Honestly, I don't know why it is I get such crazy streaks now and then out here, whereas at home I more or less behave. You can understand how it is that home life seemed different.

Will you please send me a copy of Edna St. Vincent Millay's *A Few Figs from Thistles*? I want to give it to Les for a birthday present in July. Her poems are about as dizzy as he is and as he gave me a couple of ivory and brocade things for my birthday, I need to remember his. He will have left Changsha before then, but will be in Peking. I never was in such a situation before as he will leave in five weeks or so and I may never see him again. He goes on the theory that lovely things never last. I tell him perhaps he's right if he has made up his mind to it beforehand. I would much prefer to be in love in a respectable way like Bob, though this is very exciting while it lasts. I wish there were another girl here as a bit of a safety valve, but lacking such I use you and hope you don't mind.

I haven't bobbed my hair yet though I've cut off the whole back of my head so I have left just enough to make a couple of cute little bumps in the back. Even that is warmish as our thermometers are over 80°

---

43. "Bling" perhaps a Hatism for light- hearted, maybe inebriated, enthusiastic walk. Bund is an embankment or causeway.

already. If I do the Delilah[44] act again I shall tell you, but shall not inform the family on the theory that what they don't know won't hurt them.

My vacation has been postponed until September so I have all summer to swelter in and to live with the Chinese nurses where I shall move after college closes the middle of June. I'm also going to study Chinese there hoping to learn to read and write a little. I feel like a terrible ignoramus.

We're going to try swimming this evening but as the river has just risen about 10 feet, I'm afraid it will be too swift. Perhaps we shall go riding instead. When the river

Paddy Archer

current is less, I'm going rowing with a Dutchman in the APC (Asiatic Petroleum Company) in the 2-oared shell. As my friend Paddy says at the end of a letter, "Up the rebels! Thine!"

June 3, 1926 ~ Changsha

Dear Mother,

As the Sunday School song goes, "Sunny June Has Come Again" and if May is supposed to have been the hottest month of the summer and it's finished, I shall have no trouble in staying through until September when I shall get a fur coat and head for Java I think to get warm. I wonder just how much there is to this stuff about the sunspots affecting our climate. Anyhow it has happened the last two months; the first half of the month is warm, edging onto hot, but after the full moon, each night is cloudy, really a bit cool to go for a boat ride or any of those dispensations of the evening. However, I am not complaining for I am sure we are due for a good share of hot weather when the time comes.

---

44. Delilah: enchantress, femme fatale, siren, temptress

Still I do go out into the great outdoors just the same. Last Saturday, I went riding out in the country toward the small back river and the rice fields were beautiful. The rice has been sown and then replanted in little tufts, as it will stay until harvest. It is a green color like nothing else one ever sees, more than grass, but giving the effect of a lawn at a distance where one cannot see the individual tufts.

Looking over the flat country was like overseeing a huge estate divided into various fields and with caretakers' cottages in each section. There is something about the countryside outside the cities that is very fascinating to me, and I think explains in a large way the attraction China has for me. The river was very clear and blue and the junks were gliding along very peacefully. One who has never seen it would find it hard to appreciate the real attraction of the country

Sunday, I planned to go to Ku-san, which is a mountain across the big river about three times as far back from the shore as Yolo-san, a mountain where we often picnic. Les Walker and I were going together. He is one of the bachelors who was such a friend of Clarice's last year, a very good scout and he seems to enjoy what I also seem to enjoy.

We thought the weather would be warm so planned early, real early, which is to say to rise at 4:50 a.m. Imagine! The amusing part is we did and made the start from this side at 6:30 a.m. after breakfast and packing a lunch and all that. The joke was on us, however, as there was no sun all day and a few little showers occasionally. Nevertheless, we carried on, walking for about five hours the other side of the river to the top of the so-called mountain.

These mountains are about like the ones around South Hadley as far as size goes, but are much less thickly treed and not populated at all. There is quite a lovely bamboo grove about half way up the side with a dilapidated temple occupied apparently by a fierce dog and an old woman. We did not linger there but went on up to the top where we could see for miles and miles, and then we found a sheltered spot and rested. In my usual style, I went to sleep face up and have had a very rosy sunburn in spite of there being no real sun.

We had some reading along and what with the feed and the cold tea, which we wished had been coffee, we had a very merry day. It took 2 hours to get back the same distance and we walked right onto a sampan that sailed us across the river. It was quite a day and I have felt much refreshed and cheered ever since.

With Nell Beeby sick half the time. it means Jess Norelius and I have to take turns with the Sunday weekends, instead of the original plan of one week on and two weeks off. Therefore, a weekend really away from the whole place is a great help.

Incidentally, Sunday was the long-dreaded 30th of May when some of the people were apprehensive whether there would be any trouble. I heard the students did want to parade and have a demonstration but the city is under martial law. So they petitioned the martial law office to allow them to parade one day but they were refused. We were just as pleased and those who were there that day say that it was perfectly calm with no signs of any sort of demonstrations at all.

The American flagship came up here for the day to protect us but all they did was to call on various people and have tea here and there and then go. The students are in so bad with the soldiers, having worked up such an active anti-Wu P`ei-fu campaign here before this army came in and when they thought the army of Governor Tang was being so successful, the soldiers lose no opportunity to be mean to them. They have not harmed any of the students seriously but I believe they have slapped their wrists on several occasions, and last week a group of wounded soldiers went into a very radical and Red school here and beat up some of them.

The method and policy may be all wrong but it certainly keeps the students subdued and that is what they need, most of them, for after all many of them are children who need parental discipline more than anything else.

In one town of this province there are two factions of students out for each other's blood. I guess there are not enough foreigners or soldiers there to provide a common animosity. Anyhow, if any bunch of one crowd meets a gang of the other, they pull out their little dirks from their socks and try to stab one another. There have been several casualties. It reminds me of the days when we used to play "Knight and Squire" with wooden shields and so forth, only these kids really are taken so seriously by their elders they can do some actual harm.

Our dentist, Harry Chang, leaves tonight for Kuling where he will practice all summer and then go to either Hankou or Shanghai to practice for the winter. We had a dinner party for him at our house, though Sarah couldn't come downstairs because of running a temperature again for a few days. There were fourteen of us, and we had quite a cheery time followed by dancing at Louise Farnam's house afterward.

Harry is a good egg and I hate to see him go. There are others who hate to see him go also as he does dental work for missionaries all over the province and from many outlying districts as well. I think that if Dr. Yen made some good offer to him he would stay, but they let him go anyhow. I can't understand the psychology of Dr. Yen and some of the others in charge.

For instance, in the case of Sarah Ching, who came out for two years, at the end of the second year they all wrung their hands and begged her to stay just one year more to help them out, as otherwise her department would all slump again. So she stayed, and now at the end of the additional year, they are no nearer to having someone to take her place than they were a year ago. Again they are wringing their hands and urging her to remain in spite of her pulmonary condition.

The same thing happened with the Ear, Nose, Throat man who left last spring. They all knew he was due to go and yet no one was taken on to his place, so that department, which was flourishing, is now nothing at all, practically no cases at all. I suspect the same thing will happen to the Eye department when the head of the department goes to England. Now, we will be without a dentist, though there is a place for one. Very funny!

I received a letter from you yesterday, from Fred White with a copy of "Tell It Out" enclosed. He suggests that I teach it to small patients. I think they could learn it as easily as "Jesus Loves Me." Also, I received the Sabatini book and thank you for it. Elizabeth Henry sent me the book *Gentlemen Prefer Blondes*, which is silly but amusing.

Is it possible the voltage on the electric stove was changed without indicating so on the outside? I tried to use it the other night in the operating room where they have a transformer to change from 220 to 110 but it would not heat. I did not try it directly in the 220 for fear of burning it out and ruining it and not being able to exchange it. I heard from Dr. Braun in Hankou they have no demand for 110s so he couldn't change it for me. I shall do nothing about it until I hear from you whether it might be the right voltage after all. I have just had a notice that the black tin has come. Please thank Father for it. I shall hope to do more with the diathermy now that it is here.

My friends, the S.Y. Lis, and Dr. Tang from here are going with the Indemnity students, sailing from Shanghai on the 22nd or 24th of August—I don't remember which. I wish you could meet the Lis. They are fine. Harold may want to meet them too.

Hospital Ambulance

June 17, 1926 ~ Changsha

Dear Mother,

Mail from the Asia just came to remind me that I had better snap along with a letter to you. I am delighted the kite arrived and hope it will hold together. It's too bad they don't make them a bit more substantial but as you doubtless saw, it is tied together with bits of paper twisted into strands and pasted around the joints to be joined. It may be pasted with spit. They often are!

Imagine poor old Frank flooded with work and sending word to me that he really doesn't mean anything by it. He is a rare lad, certainly. I wish there were a few more of his kind in this section of his native land. I have wondered if he is, by chance, a Hakka. That is the tribe that Sarah Ching belongs to and is a tribe that migrated toward Canton from the reign of Mongolia years and years ago. They have kept themselves distinct from the Cantonese, speaking a different dialect entirely. Many of them have gone to Hawaii and Singapore and other islands of the Pacific and are in industries and businesslike outfits.

Frank seems to have some of their characteristics but is not as husky as some of them are. Speaking of Sarah, she is much better than she was and wonders if it is necessary to go to America after all. However, she will go if only for the rest and change. Her foster parents in Berkeley are the Reverend and Mrs. Nash. He is, or has been, president of the Divinity School where Fred Morrow just graduated. I saw a commencement program they sent her with his name included.

Sarah sails directly to San Francisco. I am sorry that she doesn't go to Seattle in that you could see her for she is a rare person and a very good scout. It is as hard to believe that she is of the same race as these peer anemic run-down, bound-fasted Chinese women as it is to think of Hilda Yen as belonging to them. She is a much huskier, hardier, practical sort of a person than Hilda, who is merely the beautiful esthetic type.

There is another of our doctors going to America on the boat with Dr. and Mrs. S. Y. Li. I think I mentioned a Dr. Tang, who graduated a couple of years ago and is going to study T.B. Then there is a Dr. Chang, the same one, by the way, who made the famous remark about his family having just come from Shandong about 400 years ago. He is a very bright chap, has been at P.U.M.C.[45] for 2 years, and is now on a Rockefeller scholarship to go to Baltimore for a year. He is an odd-looking egg with a large head and too small hats, but he certainly has a lot of brains inside his head. They sail from Shanghai on August 22 with Indemnity students. I do hope you can meet them, particularly the Lis, who are charming.

---

45. Peking Union Medical College was founded in 1906.

I've just been assigned to Louise Farnam's house for next year, to live with Jess Norelius. It's a pleasant house and well-furnished, plain and real bathtubs and all that. We ought to be very comfortable though I do not particularly care for her any more than she does for me. However, we do not disagree and have a great deal in common, after all. Nell Beeby will live with Dr. Walters in the house where I now live. For the rest of the summer, I shall sleep over in the new house where the Chinese nurses are staying.

We've been much interested in news of appointments, or lack of them. Fu Liang Chang has resigned from the Middle School and takes his family to America in a few weeks. They will stay with her parents, the Hueys, in White Plains and he will go south to study cotton and then come back to Hankou in the cotton business. I think he had begun to feel a little too trapped in a way, though everyone hates to see him go. The Hails will not go on leave this year, though it is due, so the numbers will be the same.

We wonder what it all means for the future of the place. The recommendations of the Governing Board were to the effect that no new men be appointed from home under any circumstances. We wonder if that means bachelors too, as they hardly rate as new men and are supported by undergraduate subscriptions. If no new ones come, there will be only the one left over from this year besides Charlie Keller and Frank Hutchins.

As far as I can make out, it is not a matter of the Chinese attitude toward the institution which makes them move so slowly—for everything here seems very friendly—but is a matter of lack of funds. They've cut down the budget in one aspect. that is Dr. Hume has been transferred to the medical side as Dean of the Medical School, so he will no longer be President. We wonder if he will return here. No one seems to know but they suspect that he may go to Peking to serve on the China Medical Board.

On the Medical side Dr. S.Y. Li and Dr. Ching leave, Dr. Farnam goes on furlough, and Dr. Atwater does not expect to return this year and perhaps never, depending on our future. They are trying to get doctors to sign 7-year contracts instead of four or 5-year, and I think they'll have difficulty in getting good men on these terms. Yet they are building an addition to the Medical School and a Nurses' Home that leaks, as though there is no end of money in sight!

If you want Peking rugs or anything else from Peking, do let me know as people are going up this summer and can bring things back all right.

It rains and rains here—never saw anything like it! The only compensation is that it remains cool. However, people are getting an edge badly and need a change. Doubtless, we'll have it only too soon.

June 26, 1926 ~ Changsha

Dear Hank,

I'm disappointed to hear that you are planning to desert me even before you join me. However, I must say that I don't blame you in the least for going to Paris again, especially as you know about what it will cost and have someone there at home with him so you can already make plans without waiting for an uncertainty like myself. All the same, I'm perfectly sure that you would have a marvelous time if you would come in spite of the heat and smells. There are always wars somewhere in China, but there seem to be a fair amount of murder, theft, and general strikes in other parts of the world to counterbalance it.

Of course, I'm not at all sure just when I shall be released. As it is supposed to be a three-month vacation, it would logically be left to the middle of the summer, but if they thought I would not return, they would naturally postpone it to fall, Perhaps in the latter case, I would have saved enough to come by Europe. Pipe dreams again—cheap and painless.

Bulletins from the Mann-Perkins approaching nuptials are quite exciting. The blushing bride-to-be seems gloriously happy, in which state I might confess that I envy her. It would be absolutely beautiful to have one's future reasonably determined for a change, rather than wondering where to go next, and what to do. I enjoy my independence to the full and frequently realize it has its advantages.

It's been raining like the devil here for the past two months; really raining the kind that comes down so hard it nearly knocks you over. The old river rises and rises and farmers worry a bit over their rice fields. Last year there was such a drought the rice was ruined and the whole country full of starving refugees as a result. Now it seems like there may be peril for flood. Just the same the rice fields are beautiful now—a lovely rich green color and the grain about two feet high. From up on a hill, the effect is particularly charming; there are so many ponds and rivers to be seen.

Last night, I indulged in a very exclusive little twosome picnic by the light of the moon until a very late hour, but the point of this comment still centers about the scenic effect, which was unforgettable in particular, as my partner on the picnic leaves tonight as do so many of the other people, and I am feeling very low. He goes to Peking for the rest of the summer so at least will be within reasonable writing distance, about like corresponding from Seattle to New York. I have never in my life known a person so very well in so short a time nor, I might add, cared so much, but I'm glad it's interrupted before either of us tired of the other, for that would certainly come. It's only with situations like Bob's that it may last forever, but we are not matrimonially intentioned.

However, all this is between you and me. I flatly know nothing about it and by the time I go home next year, I'll have only a lovely memory and heartache to remind me. Thus it goes. Perhaps I shouldn't mention it even to you, but it's almost too much to keep to myself.

My vacation will come in September and I'm thinking of going to Kuling. It is not very far away, only about four or five days to get there and ought to be pleasant and cool by the end of the summer. Goodness knows I'll need something after the heat of this place, which is sure to come in another month.

I've been hearing from Marjorie McKillop about coming this way late in the summer. She seems to be a bit weary of Peking and craves new sites and scenes.

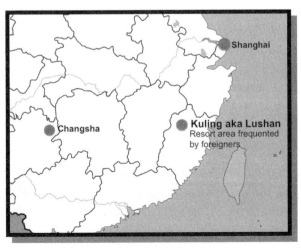

Kuling:Changsha:Shanghai

I urged her to come to Changsha but I think she will go up the Yangtze Gorges and perhaps slide over this way on her way back to Hankou. I think she would have a good time here, what with tennis and riding and swimming and rather fair company among the business people. She might even snare a job here for the winter though I'd hate the responsibility of getting her a job and having her wash out on it. I don't know what China may have done to her; how she may have changed, if at all, but I think I could stand her just the same. I might even persuade her to go to Kuling with me. A companion of any sort is better than going alone, and I think we'd get along well enough.

Three cheers for Laura. She is probably due to have five or four more babies in rapid succession according to Chinese theory.

4th of July 1926 ~ Changsha

Dear Mother,

The most patriotic thing I seem to find to do today is to write to America.

I am on duty in the hospital all day but even if I were free to go out and paint the town red and get drunk I would find my style badly cramped. There are numerous reasons. One is that so many people have left us for the summer that I would have trouble finding a crowd, let alone a congenial crowd, and the other is that we are now in the midst of a flood, and communication with the city is very damp, especially in some spots such as the American Consulate where there is about 10 feet of water, the last six inches of which are on the main floor where the offices are.

All this large amount of water is the accumulation of the last two months when it has done little else but rain and finally overflowed the banks of the Bund and began to flood the city in earnest about five days ago. Our rainfall for May was 13 inches and I am sure that June surpassed that. I think the water is about 2 feet higher than it was in the flood of 1924 just before I left.

From the top of the Hsiang-Ya Hospital one can get a very good idea of the various levels of the city and the river has certainly spread over a tremendous area of country. The island where so many foreigners live is altogether underwater and the individual houses stand up each by its wild lone—like lighthouses. Traffic in the streets is by rowboat rather than rickshaw and the resulting confusion can hardly be imagined.

Fortunately, this country is so organized one is obliged and privileged to take in neighbors or friends who are flooded or burned out, so most of the houses in the danger zone were deserted by inhabitants in plenty of time. Many of their things were left behind and now many of the houses have fallen down as the water has washed out the mud-brick foundations. It is rather a ghastly sound to hear the crash and rattle of a house collapsing into the water as the walls and roof tiles fall down. One hates to think of the awful mess that will be left in the streets and houses when the water does recede.

The worst aspects are the ruined rice fields. So much water and continuous rain has nearly finished what rice is left standing. It had reached a beautiful color and was about two feet high. I think there are places in the country farther away from here where the crop may be all right, but certainly in our immediate neighborhood it is all ruined.

The vegetable gardens are pathetic. One of the favorite occupations of the owners is to go out in tubs over what used to be the garden and with hooks and rakes try to drag up stray spinach and such. It's a rather sad sight. The remarkable part of it is how cheerful all the inhabitants seem to be. Perhaps they are too dumb to be anything else. We were crossing the railroad track at a point where there were three houses, all submerged and one of them collapsed. On the track were about half a dozen men camped, chatting together. We asked them if those were their houses and one of the younger ones said, " See that house there? (The collapsed one.) That's mine, but it's no good for living in now." At that jest they all roared with merriment. It's

Chinese peasants coping with flooding

lucky they all take it so calmly as they could certainly be miserable if they were gloomy on each count.

I sent some money to Peking for the rugs which you and Eunice asked for. I have plenty in the bank here to pay for them. The girl who will buy them is Jess Norelius, with whom I shall live next year, so she ought to have an added interest in getting good ones. I figured them at $1.75 a square foot as the US price has gone up a bit since Dwight and I bought them before. That made the total about $517 Mex. I sent her $550, and if that is more than necessary I shall have her get a small one for me with what is left.

I can't tell you how much yours will be, of course, as I am not sure whether she can get exact sizes and all that. We shall not have to pay freight as she can bring them as baggage, I think. As to how much $550 is in US, it depends on the exchange rate that, from my point of view, happens to be unfavorable at present—about $190 Mex. for $100 gold. In the fall, it will probably be less, usually somewhere around $175. That makes the difference of between $181.86 and $200 not to be sneezed at. However, we can straighten it out later. In the meantime I wish either you or Eunice would use part of the sum to pay my insurance. I shall add a postscript about it when I get home from the hospital and look it up in the correspondence with Mrs. Landon. I should like to have it paid for a year, which amounts to about $80, I think.

This rain has served one good purpose—to keep the weather cool. It has been really cool this past week, enough for one thickness of blanket even for me. I am not a bit mad, as I am very sure it will warm up enough later in the summer to make up for it. I am thinking of going to Kuling for September, but have made no definite plans. They say it can be very beautiful up there then, and I feel I should go somewhere cheap. I have heard from Marjorie McKillop, the girl from Seattle, who came with Miss Hunter a year ago. She is thinking of coming down this way this summer. I am urging her to come here for a visit at least, not that I think Changsha can qualify as a summer resort, but it would be a change from the North, and that is something.

The Winfield McLeans sent me their Fenchow paper with a memorial to Watts Pye. I haven't perused it very thoroughly, I must confess.

Railroads In Chaos

July 16, 1926 ~ Changsha

Dear Mother,

I'm not sure when mail will leave this one-horse town but as there is a possibility it will go out this afternoon I shall get this letter in this morning. The trouble is the railroad is disconnected between here and Yueyang, so nothing goes through to Hankou by rail. Then the river was so high for a while the boats were very irregular. Now things are upset by the arrival of soldiers from the South, and fighting between here and Tungting Lake[46] They fire so crazily they have hit some of the passenger boats and they have taken to using the boilerplate protection they had up four years ago. As a result, the boats are a bit leery of passing by the fighting, and our mail is a very uncertain matter. Occasionally, it comes in and every now and then it leaves. So it goes.

We have changed Governors again, though in fact the man, General Ye Ting, who has been here for a few months was never really the official Governor, the seals and all that being in the possession of his predecessor who was camping out down south of the province, collecting men and money from Canton. Last Saturday General Ye Ting and his men suddenly packed up and departed. Rumor was, Tang was coming

---

46. Also known as Dongting Lake; a large, shallow lake in northeast Hunan Province and a flood-basin of the Yangtze River.

back again and General Wu P`ei-fu had not been supporting General Ye Ting enough.

Sunday morning early I went riding out on the military road toward the South past the barracks to see what I could see. Again I was disappointed and somewhat relieved to find nothing to be seen. The barracks were as deserted as last year's bird nest and few soldiers in evidence. They looked a bit harassed and packing fierce-looking guns.

Dongting Lake:Changsha:Shanghai

In the afternoon, when Louise Farnam and I were resting on the porch, they started to fight about half a mile back of the North railroad station. It sounded quite businesslike for a while, especially when some shots went whizzing past our house. One went through the hospital third floor porch corner, one on the Branches' roof, and one on the Rollins' servant's quarters. Otherwise, we had no trouble directly. It lasted about half an hour, and has started to clear out some General Ye Ting soldiers who had lingered behind. Tang's men had come in great swarms on the southbound railroad branch and some by junk. They are now in the barracks occupied by each of the armies in turn and they have now taken to performing during in the evenings on the road past the Hsiang-Ya Hospital. They do some very businesslike looking drilling, lying down on their stomachs and clinching their guns while the officers go skidding by on mean-looking little sawed-off ponies with all the dignity in the world.

Just the same, I think they could do a bit of damage if they were to begin putting bona fide cartridges into their guns. They do the humorous marching stunt where the officer sings a measure and then they all chant it over after him to keep time. It reminds me of "Mildred" Kingsbury and "The Old Oaken Bucket."

I wrote Fred Babbitt the other day in answer to a letter he and his Sunday school class had sent me in which I told about the capture of some soldiers in Bill Rollins' basement. I shall not repeat the account Bill himself told in the *Quarterly*, which comes out in September.

Our great big old head coolie, known as "Goliath," got in quite bad with the Tang soldiers, having taken in some of General Ye Ting's soldiers and selling their guns. He was captured last evening and taken off to Headquarters. Ralph Powell, who is about half his size, went along to protect him, with Dick Leavens bringing up the rear. When last seen they were gathered in a temple not far from here, which they are using for officers quarters and all were drinking tea and smoking cigarettes and, I imagine, having a great deal of chin music.

The weather is becoming quite warm, but not as hot as I have known it by any means, or as hot as it will doubtless be later on. The thermometer is between 85° and 90° in the house most of the time, but all day we have a breeze. It usually dies down by evening and then we use the electric fans and all are happy. The nurses' home where I am now sleeping is decently cool at night so I have no trouble sleeping, and sometimes go so far as to cover only a sheet over me before morning. I do thrive on the weather and feel no qualms at all about staying here until the 1st of September. I have no very definite plans yet as to where I shall go then, though I still expect to go to Kuling if possible. After all, it is not so much where to go as just to get away from here for a change.

We are all glad the change of administration in the city came when the students were away on vacation, as the southern element is very Red and posts all sorts of lurid posters against Wu P`ei-fu and all his henchmen. The general populace does not care a great deal about who is in power as long as they have their rice to eat, and I must say it is very difficult to work up any very powerful convictions as to the merits of either side. The students, however, are of more flammable material and they eat this propaganda stuff alive. They may have something to say if the South stays in power until school opens again this fall.

I have just acquired a rather amusing souvenir. We have had one of General Ye Ting's soldiers in the hospital for several weeks. He was discharged this morning, but left behind him all his identification tags and his hat so no one would know he had been on that side. I suppose he will go out and join the South now. In the crown of his hat is a packet containing his calling cards, one of which I enclose for Frank's benefit. His collar tabs and sleeve bands I shall save for the amusement of them. Perhaps Burns would like the hat to show his little friends! It is a funny business in some ways.

July 21, 1926 ~ Changsha

Dear Hank,

The enclosed little memento means just what you'd suspect; that has gone too and I am now shorn and clipped. All I ask is, please do not tell any of my family. Having neither relatives nor fellow residents on the premise, I feel fairly sure the terrible sin will not filter through to 1305 [47] from here. So do refrain from mentioning it to any of them, won't you? They probably will find out eventually but they might as well learn later and spare themselves any distress in the meantime. No point in making anyone miserable unnecessarily. It is grand and cool and if I can ever have it trimmed so that it won't look chewed, I'll be thankful. The old boy who cuts it has the best intentions in the world and does rather well on some people, but it always looks rotten after the first time so I'm not complaining. Cost 10¢ anyhow and he came to the house!

Two doctors, men, say that it looks better than before and the wife of one doctor, who pleaded with me not to and assured me I would look terrible, never even noticed it for about ten minutes, and then conceded that it didn't look as badly as she'd feared. What she meant was that it didn't look as badly as she'd hoped because she had hers cut several years ago and looked so awful that she hates having anyone else look all right. I'll send you some snaps if I get any good ones just to show how really elegant I am.

I was driven to the point of creating some form of excitement to drive dull care away. My boyfriend left on June 26 and the bottom certainly dropped out of things for a while. It's decidedly disconcerting to have been with a person so continuously, particularly after sundown

---

47. Short reference for the family home in Seattle. A large home still standing (2011) on Seattle's Capitol Hill.

in all sorts of different places, until much later than I dare confess, and then suddenly have it end. One consolation is I've had plenty of time to make up sleep, which has taken me nearly to the present time to accomplish. Another is he's obliging enough to send along lovely letters cheering me considerably.

What a hectic life we do lead sometimes!

The only young gentleman left on the premises now is girl-shy since his fiancée ditched him last year. He's been living this year with a man whose wife—of course, you know about it—was Eleanor Keller's spouse so his environment hasn't been favorable. However, I pried him loose to go swimming the other night after he'd reneged on riding and hiking. We went about 9.30 and took a sampan from the embankment way out into the river where we fell in, much to the boatman's consternation. The crazy foreign devils have no sense anyhow.

The water was almost too warm, but the air was cool so we were delightfully refreshed. We had worn clothes over our suits so coming out we just put them on again over our wetness. The effect was most remarkable because as we walked home, increasingly water-soaked into our outside clothes, it felt quite amazing.

Frank said he'd have trouble explaining to his houseboy how he got so wet from shoulders to knees still keeping his feet dry. It was great fun and we're repeating it again soon. Meanwhile, I go on a very stylish launch picnic swimming party this evening starting at six and returning goodness knows when. There's quite a jolly crowd of business people left in port for the summer, though I haven't seen much of them because of a flood that separated us and submerged their houses. We're awfully lucky in the weather as we've had only about 2 weeks of really hot weather 86°-96° in the house and then we had a breeze. It's the sort of summer weather that exactly suits me and I don't mind the thought of staying through August a bit.

What would you say if I were to join you in Europe next summer as long as you won't condescend to join me in China? Travel through Suez is much cheaper, comparatively, than across the Pacific, and I really might do it. Ponder on it anyhow. Do tell me about Bob's wedding, won't you. I tried to send a cable of congratulations but found the telegraph wires to Hankou are out of order and it would have to go part way by mail. There is fighting just below us on the river so our boat service is very uncertain, perhaps a boat a week and maybe not. I'd like Bob to know that I had noble intentions anyhow.

We've had another change of power here in Changsha–Hunan. Wu P`ei-fu and his representatives departed bag and baggage, gunboats included, when word came that troops were coming in large numbers from Canton under his predecessor.

There was one little flurry of fighting one afternoon, cleaning out a few leftovers. It all suited us well, not that their battles are so intense, but they do hit people every now and then whether they mean to or not. The southern troops now here are a well-traveled, weather-beaten outfit, some from Kwangtung and some from provinces. Their officers are quite neat and snappy and each General has a Russian advisor.

Russian support is all with the Cantonese element and they seem to know about warfare. I wonder whether Feng will not join them to oust Wu P`ei-fu and Chang Tse Lin from the North. It's all so problematical, one can't predict. Probably Jane knows more about it than any of us here do. Just tune in some night when she's broadcasting on "Bolshevism in China," or something of that sort. Maybe she doesn't descend so far from the heights of Hu Shih[48].

July 31, 1926 ~ Changsha

Dear Mother,

I must get this letter off so that Dr. Faster can take it to Hankou to be mailed. I am just not sure how the mails leave Shanghai but with our boat service not altogether certain it is better to get if off this evening.

There is quite a delegation leaving this evening for vacations, including Dr. Roster and Dr. Hellins and the Branch family. Miss Gage is also officially on her vacation but plans to stick around here for August and perhaps go to the conference in Peking in September.

They are great ones for having conferences here, not as many as at home even so, I think, and yet they seem to come rather often. This is the same sort of national medical affair. Miss Gage had expected to dash all over the country this month and visit various hospitals in different places but now says what is the use of doing that when she can

---

48. A Chinese philosopher, essayist and Taiwan Chinese Nationalist diplomat and scholar.

sit by her electric fan in her own house with her books and whatnot and be comfortable. I say, why stick at home, fan or no fan, when there is the opportunity of going off somewhere for a few weeks? I surmise that that is due to the slight difference in our ages that regulates our points of view. The additional argument in favor of going away is we have about $160 paid toward our expenses, making it not much more expensive than living at home. To be sure, I have not yet decided where to go myself for September. I have nearly a month to decide.

Did I tell you my delightful little Scottish friend, the ship captain, who came through Seattle last year and entertained the young Eunices with tales of Easter Island, is now on a boat from Hankou to Shanghai? I have just written him to know just when he leaves Hankou near the 1st of September so I might be able to take the same steamer as far as a Yangtze River city Kiukiang[49] if I go to Kuling. I think that would be good fun.

Guangxi Zhuang:Changsha:Hong Kong:Shanghai

I am still living with Louise Farnam, as I think I wrote before. She is having the house painted in sections so we move from room to room in the greatest confusion and her sleeping porch looks just like a New York tenement. It is a pleasant house and great when it is in order again. That will be soon I hope. We have been living rather casually with only one servant for this month. He is a rickshaw coolie by profession and served us toast, fruit, G. Washington coffee, and dry cereal with the greatest care and clumsiness. For tiffin, we had Chinese chow sent over from the nurses' kitchen, and for dinner we went over to Miss Gage's and ate in great style at 8 or 8:50. For tea we

49. Now know as Jiujiang

went wherever there seemed to be any, sort of tea tramps as it were. All the same it was less expensive and good fun.

Louise Farnam is a rare soul, a PhD as well as an M.D., a person with lots of brains and yet an awful nut in many ways. She has amused me to the greatest degree, surprising her considerably. I think she has been living with an adolescent sense of humor and it rather pleases her to have one appreciate her little witticisms, as many of them are rather adolescent.

She has the most informal way of strolling about with very few clothes on, a habit which pleases me immensely particularly in this hot weather. Her house is off the main beat, so to speak, so one is in comparative safety particularly at this season. I sleep in the dormitory with the Chinese nurses but have not had much chance to see them because I am busy most of the day and am through dinner rather late in the evening. I may see more of them during the coming month when I have dinner at Louise's.

I study Chinese for an hour every day with a Mr. Cheng. He is quite a stylish young man who had incipient TB and was in the hospital for about four months when I first came. Now he is staying at home in the old TB hospital just beyond our compound, and a very easy walk from the hospital. We do not use a book but just sit and talk about typhoid and TB and dysentery and all sorts of such topics, which do not fit me very well for dinner party conversation. He is very accurate and careful in his pronunciation both in Chinese and in the small amount of English he knows. He told Louise once, in Chinese, he could come any time to give her a lesson, "because," said he in Chinese, " I am a (in English) celibate." She was much taken back.

Last time I went to have a lesson I wore a thin blouse of green I had made to go with the separate white skirts. He raised his eyebrows and remarked in Chinese, 'Miss Smith, you are beautiful. Your dress is like (in English) dragon fly's wings." Now, I ask you, isn't that poetic? I was surprised, to say the least.

We have as a patient now a Mr. K.C. Chen, who is none other than one of the Chinese who lived with your friend Mrs. Paine. I wish you would tell her next time you write her. He is in the Hunan University presently. It is a government school but I don't know just how it ranks.

I think he has held various kinds of educational and political jobs in the past. I judge he is rather an oily guy, like most of the rest of them; but he is very pleasant to meet. He was in the hospital last fall for a herniatomy and has had a recurrence, and why he is in again now.

I did not know he was the one who was with Mrs. Paine until I asked him where he came from and where he had been educated in America. When he said "Ann Arbor," I knew it must be the same one. He made the same remark K.Y. Wang and F. C. Tang used to make and that is that he really should write to Mrs. Paine. I assured him he certainly should. I hope he does, but I doubt it.

He is known here as "Golden Chain" but how he gets it I don't know unless it is some sort of perversion of his name Chen and his first name, two of which I have heard and neither of which sound the least bit like Golden.

There has been a bit of excitement around here lately in the unearthing of an old tomb. At least they think it was a tomb that was never used. After the flood some people down toward the river from here were digging a place where their house had been to rebuild their house, which had been washed away by the flood. Suddenly they found they had dug into a hole and on digging mud from a mound found it was a doorway, which led into a regular house below. The doorway itself seemed quite low but the rooms are normal size. I think there are about six of them, two of which were sealed up. Of course the people were scared to death and sealed it up again, but more adventurous souls dug it up again and went inside on short expeditions to peek around. It was pitch dark there but someone strung up lights and then charged admission to go inside and look. They say that after all there is nothing to see except bare walls. The material which it is made of, however, discloses its age that is put at about 1500 years ago, Han Dynasty[50].

Then Changsha was quite a famous place and there were great deeds done here. Many great men lived here and I presume this tomb was built for someone who had his head taken off before it was finished, and then being so near the river it has gradually been buried in various floods until no one knew it was there any more. The bricks are quite large and about the weight and consistency of lead. On one, the

---

50. The Han Dynasty (206 BC – 220 AD) was the second imperial dynasty of China.

thinner sides are various designs that must have made it quite beautiful at the beginning. Unfortunately there is no Archaeological Society to preserve it intact and no city government to protect it so anyone is going in and taking bricks and all that sort of thing. Not to be outdone in vandalism, I am getting a couple bricks myself. I think they might be rather valuable if sent to the right place. An archaeologist like Jan's spouse might be glad to buy a Han Dynasty brick for his museum. Our engineer found a coin there that they traced in a coin book and decided was 1100 A.D. I should think that might date the place itself. I do feel how young and callow is our own good USA when any coolie can casually go out and pick up things in his own backyard that are 1000 years old.

I presume by this time the rush of weddings is over. I should like to have been there to throw a couple of shoes apiece to each of them and give them my blessing. I almost sent a cable to Bob Mann just for fun, but the telegraph wires are down between here and Hankou and I decided it was not worth the risk because it might arrive a few days after the event and they had gone faraway to Tacoma or somewhere. I think I'll leave the matter of wedding presents until I can bring something home myself. It is hard to send anything decent through the mail without the problem of duty at the other end.

There is fighting down the river according to news we receive but it still remains quiet here. Did I write you about the Kwangsi troops who have been drilling on the Maloo outside the hospital and in the hospital grounds too, singing do-re-mi songs? They really use those words and it sounds too queer for anything. Sometimes it is in antiphonal style with the leader singing a phrase and then the men singing it back and sometimes it is all together when they are marching. It is quite effective but they keep very slow time.

Lately those Kwangsi[51] (Guangxi) men have moved on and a gang of Hunan men from the southern part of the province have come in their place. They are a tough-looking crew, not particularly fierce, but just rough coolie kind. Even their officers have not the class of real southern men. Strange to say we have had more trouble with those

---

51. Guangxi, formerly transliterated as Kwangsi, is an autonomous region (Guangxi Zhuang Autonomous Region) of the People's Republic of China.

later ones than with their predecessors. Some of them have run off with doors and benches and so forth, strange loot, but not so strange when one realizes the poor things are quartered in a place without enough beds and they have to sleep on the ground otherwise.

Jess Norelius should be back next week and I hope will bring the rugs with her. I shall be eager to see them and if they are as good looking as Dr. Walters brought, they will be fine.

I gave a letter of introduction to the father of one Chinese doctor, who will arrive on the same steamer with the indemnity students the 1st of September. It is Dr. Chang who graduated from here several years ago and has been studying at Peking ever since. He is a bright man but not what you would call handsome. I do hope Father can meet them, that is, he and Dr. S.Y. Li. The latter plans to go right on to the East but Dr. Chang would like to linger if there is anything for him to see in Seattle. It is his first trip to the USA

Louise Farnam has just suggested I go with her to Shanghai in September and then to nearby Hangchow[52] (Hangzhou). There is the "Bear" phenomenon every autumnal equinox when the tide rushes up through a narrow place in a wall about 20 feet high.

The Chinese think it's great and the lake there is beautiful. I should really like to go and may arrange it for the last of the month.

Hangzhou:Shanghai:Changsha

---

52. Hangzhou, formerly Hangchow, is the capital and largest city of Zhejiang Province in Eastern China.

August 8, 1926 ~ Changsha

Dear Mother,

I have had mail from you lately from two boats and it begins to seem as though we are not so far from civilization after all. When we go without mail for over a week as we have at times this summer, it seems as though we are quite isolated. I am glad you had a pleasant trip to Spokane. With no Eunice and no Frank it seems a good time to go tripping off around the country. From what Father says, my friend Grace Schively must be quite capable of carrying on at the office. She has written me, she seems to enjoy it and manages to keep busy.

I finally received a letter from Oconomowoc about rugs for the Austins. Unfortunately, they were a bit late in putting in their order as the friend who was to get them has been back for over a week, and the other one who is bringing the rugs for you and Eunice arrives today. However, there are still some people I know in Peking and so I am asking Les Walker to buy them for me, and Dr. Greene to bring them back as far as Hankou when he returns from a medical conference in September. I can pick them up there on my way home from vacation so all ought to be all right.

They ask for dark blue ones, but I am taking exception to their choice of colors and asking him to get a taupe color. My reason is Dr. Walters just came back with some beautiful rugs in a soft, warm, sort of mouse color with Chinese design at the sides. I really think they will be better for small feet to run about than blue, and are quite as handsome. If, by any chance, they do not want that color at all, I might be able to buy some more through friends at Chinese New Year time and keep these for myself. I almost wish that might be the case to get one 9 x 14 and two 3 x 9s to fit their living room.

That takes another $350 out of my bank account but strange to say I can stand it, and shall ask them to send whatever the real amount is to you so that it can be for me rather than change it into $ Mex and then into gold at a loss. I hope between now and next summer to buy my ticket home so that I will not have to use any money I may have accumulated at home. I shall save that for my old age, for the Old Folks Home. On the other hand, I might use it to buy my ticket back here again if I decide to return.

I am really making vacation plans now and think I shall go to Kuling the first of the month, at least. Louise Farnam has a friend joining her about mid-month and they will continue through Europe and home. I may join forces with them on their way downriver and go to Shanghai and Hangchow. I hesitate on the grounds of expense, but may decide I can afford it all right. We hear from people in Hankou and Shanghai they are receiving desperate reports of conditions in Changsha. If they hear things of that sort in China, I wonder how they may have grown by the time they reach America.

Fortunately, you have had enough experience with the discrepancies between fact and rumor of goings-on here that you would not be alarmed by newspaper reports. In fact, I have never felt more peaceful and calm than at present, and the soldiers give us no trouble at all. Occasionally, they are a bit annoying as when some of them stole a couple of doors to sleep on, as they were quartered in places having no signs of beds at all.

A niece of Mrs. Ling, who is visiting her now, remarked the other day—after we had heard some rumors of trouble to the South—she had never before realized the safety of life in America until she came to China, and I replied I had never realized the safety of life in Changsha until I lived in America again.

I quoted robberies, holdups and auto accidents as proof against her very thin arguments of rumored looting in either place. I really think she had to admit I had some grounds for my opinion. I may be fooled one of these days when our houses are burned about us or something, but in the night I go from the city alone in a rickshaw and go every evening to the Nurses' home with nothing to disturb me but dogs.

Today is a sort of Groundhog Day with the Chinese. If it rains today, it will rain for a week or ten days, and if it doesn't, goodness knows when we will have rain. We agreed it had done enough in the early summer to last for some time. but they do need some in the country.

I would not object but we are getting along very nicely with the bright warm days with a breeze. To be sure, our mountain Yolo-san is beginning to look a little brown on top, a condition it usually develops in July or earlier. The actual rainfall for June was 19 inches I am told. That is quite a neat amount, and enough to last some places for many months if carefully distributed. I really think it does not rain so much in dear old Seattle.

By the time I come back from vacation all will be under way for the fall. That is the time I like to come, rather than having vacation early and returning for the summer heat. I am lucky at it. I suppose by the time this reaches you, Frank will be back from Alaska. What were his final grades for the term? Anything as disgracefully low as a B?

August 17, 1926 ~ Changsha

Dear Mother,

As mail will leave today, I must get this off on the afternoon collection. We have suddenly become very busy so I have not much time it seems. Fortunately, Miss Norelius came home last Saturday so I had the weekend off duty and it did seem queer to be out of uniform for a day and a half. I had been sticking rather close to the job though not necessarily in the hospital all the time. She had significant trouble getting back as she was on the train that was held up by a washout flood between Hankou and Peking. It delayed her five days, part of which were spent in going back toward Peking, and part on the train in the city of Chengchow[53] and part in the city itself at a Mission there, while her train went back to Peking and then returned again. It was a disagreeable mess and yet she doesn't seem to be any the worse for wear. Also, she brought with her the rugs I had asked her to buy for you and Eunice.

The rugs were more expensive than I had estimated but are beautiful and well worth even at a greater cost. The large one for Eunice is 8½ x 10½, blue-figured background and a tan border with a cutout design of blue in the middle of the four sides. Then there is one 3 x 5½ with a bamboo design running up the two long sides and a sort of lantern in the middle of the long sides. A smaller one, 3 x 5, has a blue background and a rather colorful border of tan, blue and rose color. The smallest is 2 x 6 and is somewhat like the one she already has; that is, it is a sort of picture of a bridge and a tree and a big bird. Then the one for you, which you wanted, a 6 x 6, she could not get, but did buy one 7 x 7, which is round. It has a tan background and a design all over in blue. It is very

---

53. The capital and largest city of Henan Province in north-central China.

handsome and would look well in the reception room rather than in the hall.

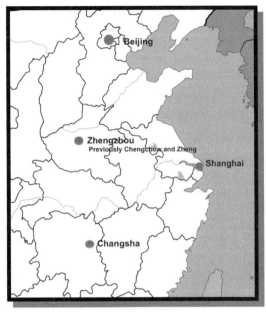

Shengzhou:Changsha:Shanghai:Beijing

She could not get one 6 x 9 as you requested because they did not have that size on hand and she did not have any money left. If you want smaller ones of a different size, she can have them sent to me by parcel post from Peking at any time. I have not had an invoice yet but shall expect it soon. Exchange is very good now for buying Mex but I think you had probably better keep the money in gold anyhow, especially as I do not know the exact amount at this time.

Speaking of funds, I think you asked me about price of my linen. Any that you want to take you may charge yourself half the price that I marked on it and it will be about right.

I am thinking of trying to get apples through the Gilberts in Yakima. I shall write to them with an idea I have about it and suggest they send the bill to you, so if you receive such you will know what it is all about.

We are overrun with soldiers these days and everyone predicts a fierce battle soon, probably not here but north of here somewhere. Certainly the men are not drilling here in such numbers as they were. They pass through the city rather quickly. They have just taken to commandeering various missions in which to sleep. Last night, we had about 300 in the Yale dormitory and they were in the Presbyterian and the American Church missions.

We have had no trouble with them at all as we have treated them in a calm and polite manner, but other places that have opposed them have had a bit of argument. We anticipate no trouble for the present, but we do . . . .now just how it will be if they do fight near here, and when the students come back I don't know how they will behave.

The Cantonese General Chiang Kai-shek[54] is a Communist, which accounts for the using of foreign property, as he is anti-foreign, and anti-Christian in theory at least. Some gang of soldiers or bandits or something grabbed the man in charge of the APC (Asiatic Petroleum Co.) installation here last week and put him in a sack and took him outside the city and demanded $60,000 for him.

The soldiers (bandits) have reduced the ransom to $20,000 and have not yet come to terms that I know of. It brings that sort of thing rather close to have one of our fellow-citizens treated so. No one seems to know just who has taken him, or what the government will do about it, though the new Governor seems inclined to do nothing and does not recognize the group who has taken the old boy.

I don't know just how it will come out. Some of our Chinese staff say it is much harder for them being associated with foreigners, and yet being Chinese, than it is for the

Chiang Kai-shek

Asian Petroleum Company Headquarters

54. Chiang Kai-shek was the leader of the Nationalist Party, the Kuomintang (KMT), from 1925 until his death in 1975, and a close ally of Sun Yat-sen.

foreigners themselves. I can believe it is so, as they are called "foreign slaves," which pains them more than our being called "foreign devils." I think the southerners, if victorious, may commandeer our hospital and staff for their use.

At present we have quite a few of their men—medical cases, no wounded. Plenty of dysentery and some typhoid. They've had much cholera in their troops and have brought it to this city and other cities nearby. There is a cholera hospital in the city so we do not take any cases here as we did four or five years ago. It keeps us very busy indeed. One of our graduates has succumbed to the temptation of joining the army as a doctor and it is hard for them not to take an opportunity to earn five or six times their present salary. I fear there are plenty of promises and perhaps not so much cash.

I understand the Blacks may come this fall. If they are delayed before this fall because of unsettled conditions, they will find it much more serious now. The flood and not the thousands of soldiers has affected the food supply and there is prospect of a rice shortage for the winter. If the South stays here, there is almost sure to be some trouble with students and their Communistic tendencies. There are all sorts of rumors, even as near as Hankou, as to the impossibility of getting to Changsha, etc., so it is possible it is even worse in Shanghai where they were advised about it before. Even so, we carry on in the same sort of way as usual, unexciting and very warm.

August 23, 1926

Things are getting very interesting here in the political line. You probably hear about it nearly when we do, but I refer to the Hunan events. I have told about the southern troops going through and they seem to be walking right along, reported today to have taken Yueyang. That moves the real encounter still farther away unless Wu P`ei-fu comes to the rescue with large numbers of northern troops to keep them from Hankou.

The general opinion is the merchants and influential men in Hankou will not allow the southern troops to take that city; they'll buy them off first. I wonder whether these men can be bought. I presume so, though while they have support from Russia, as is the general opinion,

I suppose they wouldn't be much impressed by the money from Hankou. The boss of the whole shebang is here now, Marshal Chiang Kai-shek, the successor to Sun Yat-sen[55] in Canton. He arrived at 2 a.m. one day midst a terrific din of firecrackers and cannon and shouting populace. He holds street meetings frequently and addresses large crowds all the time. I don't know just how much of a Communist, anti-foreign, anti-Christian he is, but those are the doctrines of his party at least.

Sun Yat-sen,
Known as the Father Of Modern China

There have been no demonstrations to prove any of these points so far but there may be if they are victorious for the winter. Our relations with them have been so pleasant and the members of their army who have been in the hospital are so very decent that we are in danger of losing our neutrality, unofficially at least.

One interesting detail about the officers who have been here, some thirty or so within the last few weeks, is none of them are native Cantonese. They come from nearly every other province of China but Canton. Many of them seem well-educated, speaking English or, in one case, French. The latter gentleman had studied French "à Paris," he said.

It may be they are merely trying to get in well with the hospital, but it really seems as though they are just naturally decent and well-behaved. They do not have the domineering manner one might expect, particularly from a conquering army. They have a tired lot of different uniforms from green with shorts to tan, light blue or dark blue, some

---

55. Sun Yat-sen (12 November 1866 - 12 March 1925) was a Han Chinese doctor, revolutionary and political leader. As a pioneering Nationalist, Sun is frequently referred to as the "Father of the Nation" by both the Republic of China and the People's Republic of China.

with spiral puttees, some with leather and some with long straight trousers. Their hats are most amusing.

We almost never see the General Feng style (jockey cap with visor) like a beehive. They wear more regular (army style) hats but those from Kwangsi have no wire in the crown so they resemble tam-o'-shanters, somewhat, and the Cantonese have very wide crowns gathered underneath into a band. Their button is of the Guominjun faction[56], a many-pointed white star on a blue background. The same appears on their flag, white star on blue background in its center and the rest of the flag, red.

We never see the striped Republic flag anymore. We have a Revolutionary flag flying from the Medical School. It is so easy to change one's political sympathy and loyalty. At least one is not deserting one cause for another, though these Canton people do have the name of working for the good of their country.

Apart from patients and visits from inspecting officers, encounters have been few but important. Last Sunday, a call came from Marshal Chiang; he, to have a dentist come to see his teeth. As our dentist has gone, the call was referred to Louise Farnam, who in turn passed the buck to Phil Greene, who said he would go if Louise would go too as his assistant. They set off in grand style with all their instruments and equipment and had to wait a while for him to appear. They were served with coffee and tea and allowed to sit in a very hot room where they both glowed through all their clothes.

While they were waiting various people kept coming in and going out and finally one man in shirt sleeves and suspenders came in and shook hands with them in a businesslike way. Phil, who is inclined to be YMCA-ish beamed at him and asked, "And what is the gentleman's name?" The man replied, "Chiang," just like that. It makes a lovely story in the telling considering the style of Chinese expression Phil used. It rates with some amusing Calvin Coolidge stories. At least he doesn't surround himself with pomp and ceremony.

---

56. The Guominjun military faction was sympathetic to Sun Yat-sen's Kuomintang regime in Guangzhou; however, due to geographic isolation, they operated independent of one another.

I had an interesting experience last week buying sugar. Our house and Dr. Walters' decided to buy a case of table salt and a bag of cooking sugar, about 300 lbs., worth $50. We sent the coolie to bring it but just as he was leaving the South gate the sugar was confiscated by Student Union pickets and taken to their headquarters. There they parked it and refused to let the coolie bring it because it was English goods in the possession of a Chinese and there's a boycott on English things. They overlooked the fact it was purchased by Americans and is essentially a Chinese product as it is refined in Canton and shipped from there through a British firm.

They are really taking food from their own mouths when they boycott it. Anyhow, our coolie came back all excited because they had called him a foreign slave, which is a terrible insult. So Dr. Walters and I went to the headquarters to get it back. I was glad for the experience though it wasn't the pleasantest in the world. There were many hectic and perspiring youths dashing about here and there and many short-haired women government school students lolling about.

We were taken into an inner room and there interviewed. They just asked our nationality, whether we'd paid for the sugar, for proof it was ours, and many more senseless inquiries. They then assured us we couldn't have an answer before the next day or possibly in three days. They said they were holding a meeting, hoped to go to the front, want to fight, and please go home now.

Our "leader" was a hard-boiled-looking customer who had no time to even look over our bill. Every now and then someone would rush out into the room's middle and announce something to which no one paid the slightest attention and then someone would ring a bell or strike a gong, with the same effect on the gathering. It was quite an "*Alice in Wonderland*" sort of business.

They finally ushered us to the outer room where our sugar was parked. On one wall there was a frieze of life-sized lurid pictures of Shanghai "victims"—the students killed last year. They were the most horrible looking collection. The next day, Phil Greene went down to rescue it for us and said the place was very quiet but orderly; the conclusion being, Ota and I were hysterical females. They may have all gone off to the front, though I should think so apparently well-organized an outfit as this army would hate to have a crowd of disorganized, hysterical students in their midst.

Some Red Cross workers came to look over the hospital and to start an army hospital across the road from us. The leading woman had on a man's uniform, which was not so startling in this land of trousered women. The doctor in charge was a graduate of a German University and has a German spouse. Louise was quite pleased with him. Phil committed another *faux pas* of a harmless nature by introducing Louise to the doctor as "Herr Doktor Farnam."

I am at present on the *S.S. Siangtan* trying to go on a vacation. Fighting downriver has interrupted their schedule and we were scheduled to start last night. However, they declared martial law at 9 p.m. so no freight could be loaded and we're still in the port of Changsha. It's interesting to view it from this angle. Last week the papers here said the river was mined so no boats could come or go. Just then, up came two Japanese steamers from Hankou. They hadn't heard the rumor, and next morning two British boats and the American gunboat left for downriver so this one came in. That is what is known as "calling their bluff." They're afraid soldiers or arms will be smuggled in—a legitimate fear—and they do their best to get around it.

The British Consul here, Mr. Coates, died very suddenly the other morning. Phil was called to see him at 7 and he died on the way to the hospital. He had an axillary temperature of 107, but the autopsy showed nothing but "icterus hemorrhagic," some liver business, isn't it? Anyhow it was a great shock to the community, though he wasn't too popular, a weak-livered (perhaps a fatal) sort of person with little force, but a pleasant manner. His wife and small son were in Kuling, sad to say.

Fortunately, he had seen the rescue of Mr. Moore, the APC man who was held for ransom here for two weeks and just got him out for $5000. People had begun to wonder why he didn't seem able to do anything about it. Mr. Moore is an oldish scout of 50 or so with a Eurasian spouse. These Chinese grabbed him in the middle of the night and tied him in a sack and held him captive in a closed room without ventilation. As the weather was very hot, the poor little man was quite miserable. It was an unpleasant experience, to say the least, and no one seems to know just what the real reason for it was.

As for rugs: I've received the bill for everything and settled with the store and Miss Norelius. It's as follows:

Eunice:

8 x 10 @ $2	$178.50
5 x 5	$50.00
3 x 6	$36.00
2 x 3	$12.00

Yours:

7 x 7 @ $2.10	$102.90
	$359.40

Excess baggage	$9.15
Baskets to pack in	$6.00
Insurance	$1.54
Coolie hire	$1.40
	$18.09
	$377.19

You see the price has gone up considerably since last time we bought them. It is still going up so these will be cheaper than they'll be in another year or so probably.

At the time of buying, the exchange was about $1.90 making it worth $198.67 gold. As I figure it, your share translated into gold ($1090.90 for rug plus $5.18 your share of extra expenses) is $56.82 and the balance $141.85 for Eunice. Will you use that and enough from Eunice's to make the Life Insurance payment? As for the rest, if exchange is two to one or more favorable; that is, if Mex. is cheap, please buy $100 gold worth of Mex dollars and send to American-Oriental Banking Corporation, Shanghai for deposit to my account—dollars not teals. That will be easier than sending it and also bolster my rather depleted bank account. I can buy back in gold later when the exchange is favorable that way. If you detect I am making a little off you in this figuring of accounts, I really think you ought to grant it to me for being so clever. In any case, buy the Mex and send to the bank and keep the difference for future buys.

Example of Asian Rug (Several Still in Family Collection)

August 27, 1926 ~ Changsha

Dear Hank,

Your letter arrived today containing the pictures of Bob and bride and the account of their wedding. The one with the veil looks as though it might have been made from the other gown just by adding the veil. Both are very good. The lurid details of festivities and the wedding make me feel very far away both geographically and matrimonially. We're both dangerously near the stage where we'll have to scout for widowers and be married quietly at home to preserve the dignity of our years.

What in blazes is the matter with your Loomis friend? Is he the kind that can't see further than the end of his nose and whose taste is all in his mouth, as they say? I begin to suspect it. Something certainly ought to turn up.

As for my heart condition, so to speak, it's just adventuring with another sort of fire I never played with quite so before. He is an odd genius and the reason I wanted the Millay poems was because they echo his sentiments. He wrote a poem himself to the effect "lovely things never last." He believes it, too, though someday he'll find it is fallacious, I think. He's Les[57], that's enough, about my own size, blond, and some five or four years younger, was a teacher here, now he's nothing but a wild adventurer. Cradle snatcher, I'll tell you a secret. He's writing a novel up in Peking and when he's finished he will beat it home and catch a job.

This summer looks like the best and perhaps last opportunity to write as much as he chooses, with no interruptions. I do hope he makes something of it as it's his whole interest now and may mean a real career for him in the future. He's clever and has lots of brains but is a bit of a pagan. I'll be curious to see what sort of philosophy he writes into his novel.

I may never see him again; rather hope I don't because what could be more ghastly than an anticlimax of bald-headed and false teeth after a perfect few weeks in which we learned to know each other so well. It was all probably immoral from the standpoint of regulated society and all that—this business of taking as much that opportunity offers without a thought for tomorrow. I shan't be doing it again very soon, but in the meantime have a group of happy memories that nothing can rob me of. Thanks ever so much for the *Figs from Thistles*. Shall I send you something or the price in money? If the latter, I'll instruct my family to settle. You might be interested in his comment on it.

---

57. Apparently, Charles Lester "Les" Walker, who later became a war correspondent and writer for *Harper's* and *The New Yorker* magazines.

"Please, again, take thanks for the little Figs from Thistles. *I send you the honey of my love to eat with the first, and Time for a glove to pluck the last with. Which leads me to the last sonnet. Is it for that you sent me the book? A book of poems from a woman is always a Sphinx between covers—there's a riddle hidden about it somewhere."*

Isn't it great to be thought subtle and mysterious? Also, does it savor of "climbing the heights . . . or ever we have reached the summit?" What poetic correspondents I seem to have. I think Les is mixed in his figures. He's thinking of syrup of figs. Don't you believe so?

It's hot as the deuce here these days, over 90° all the time and no breeze. We all drip all over all the time and the poor patients are covered with prickly heat. Many of our patients are soldiers from Canton. Their troops have passed through here on their way to Hankou and seem to be having a successful time. Though they represent the Revolutionary party, the Kuomingchun, they are not actively anti-foreign or anti-Christian; in fact conduct themselves in a more friendly, businesslike, cordial fashion than any of their military predecessors. Two of our doctors went down into the city to treat Marshal Chiang himself for a toothache and were pleasantly impressed. We are in danger of turning Bolshevik if these people are fair examples of Bolshevik behavior.

One "Britisher" was captured by some Chinese and for a couple of weeks held for ransom of $75,000, which was finally reduced to $5,000 cash. After all, that is no more desperate than what happened to many people in the great and glorious USA. No one knows just who grabbed him or why, though there is probably some reason for it somewhere. It may make a good newspaper story. You may see it in the Associated Press.

I go on my vacation next Tuesday, thank God. Pardon the cussing, but I feel like it after a whole summer in this hot hole and I need a change in that so many people have been away. I shall go to Kuling for sleep and swimming. Here's hoping there'll be some.

Be sure to read *By the City of the Long Sand* by Alice Tisdale Hobart. It's all about us, not Yali but Changsha. She's the spouse of a Standard Oil boss here and I know her quite well. She has a pleasant style and has not roused any very violent antipathies among people here. They've just been transferred to Nanking within the last month.

She wrote a book called *Pioneering Where the World Is Old*, an account of their early experiences in Manchuria.

Well, Hankie[58], thanks for your letters and let's hear more from you. It won't be very long now until we'll be able to discuss it 'face to face," as the Chinese say, even though you are dashing off to Europe and leaving me.

September 6, 1926 ~ Kuling

Dear Mother,

I am triumphant, what there is around here, and it is certainly clear and fine. There's pep in the air and a good bright sun. I shall make the most of the three weeks I'm here.

I saw history in the making in Hankou. I believe that's what it would be called. Our little friends from the South, the Guominjun who were ensconced in Changsha, had continued nearly to Wuchang, the city across the river from Hankou. Coming on the boat from Changsha we saw no signs of them until we were a few hours from Hankou. Then there were a few shots fired at us, none of which came nearer than ¼ mile, according to the Captain. That was quite near enough. In Hankou there was a pervading atmosphere of expectancy. The Chinese were hurrying through the streets, bag and baggage, by foot and by rickshaw, taking their families and possessions to safety in the foreign concessions[59].

The servants' quarters in all the houses in the Concessions were filled with people and behind all their gates were rows of Chinese faces. It is just a little amusing to think the entire row and protest they make against extra-territoriality and yet when there is any trouble they all come scuttling for protection under foreign flags. They theoretically go with foreigners to be on the same basis as themselves, yet they are pathetically eager to admit they have no protection against their own people and flock to the foreign shelters in times of trouble.

At any time during the day, one could hear the constant scurry of feet through the streets, a regular Pied Piper of Hamlin sort of exodus

---

58. Pet name for friend Elizabeth Henry

59. Concession. In international law, a concession is a territory within a country administered by an entity other than the state holding sovereignty over it. This is usually a colonizing power, or at least mandated by one, as in the case of colonial chartered companies.

from the Chinese city. They said it had been much worse a few days before; rickshaws had stopped running and people were trying to transport their own possessions. What they fear is the retreating army. If the northern soldiers are defeated at Wuchang, as they probably will be, they will retreat across the river and flee through Hankou. That will mean looting and perhaps burning, as it is an old custom of soldiers to do so to prevent the invaders from enjoying their prize, I suppose.

Fortunately for us in Changsha, the changes of armies have occurred with a day's interval so there has been practically no looting. On the third morning, the siren called out the Volunteers. That is an organization of all the businessmen, foreigners of course. They all donned uniforms and were stationed throughout the Concessions, guarding American and other property.

I came across Gordon Burke and Ralph Gregory of Standard Oil in front of the American Consulate, looking rather foolish and very warm. However, in the morning there was heavy firing over in Wuchang and we could see the shells bursting over the city. It's hard to tell just what was going on and all sorts of rumors came over—the city was taken, that it wasn't taken, the South had retreated, the South was advancing, etc.

Several boats going upriver toward Changsha were back by firing and the British gunboats have had various encounters with men firing from the shore. The lion seems to be growling at them. I pity the Chinese when he begins to roar. He's had his tail twisted rather frequently and has given warning he wouldn't stand much more. This being war, he can really defend himself with guns, which we were blamed for using in Shanghai. We've had no definite news up here since I came, except a report no boats were going to Changsha, as the river is mined. We heard last week, but the boats continued to go. Now we don't know how true it is this time, but it doesn't concern me as I'm up here with no interest in returning until month's end.

Had a very simple time coming up the mountain here. Only one small row with sampan coolies. As I was ordering a chair, a large Teutonic looking individual came along and we started off together. My bearers asked if we were related. I assured them we were, so they hustled along to keep up with his chair, eight bearers against my six.

It meant there were no delays, that sometimes occur when a woman is alone, demands made for tea money, and requests she walk, and all that. It was about five hours from the boat to the house.

I am with Ruth Greene and her twin 17-month-old babies. They are wonderful and I am very fond of Ruth. However, I'm thinking of departing to a boarding house today and spare myself association with people I'll see all winter. I like them but I hate to spend my vacation amid howling infants. I'm afraid I'm getting to be an old maid.

The trains from Peking to Hankou are so interrupted by soldiers being transported; I wonder how the Austins' rugs are coming from Les who bought them last month! We're hoping for good transportation by the end of this month.

I was very amused by the Sunday school contest. I'm writing to Mrs. Pontius. I had a letter from Fred White but he didn't mention flying here!

September 11, 1926 ~ Kuling

Dear Mother,

I've been looking around here for some small thing to send you in an envelope for your birthday, and have finally in despair resorted to the old faithful handkerchiefs. There are numerous very attractive ones here and they are not very expensive. I enclose two with love and best wishes, just to show you I remember.

There are some lovely things to buy here and I've spent quite a neat sum altogether but have good things to show for it: rice pattern china like Katherine has, some of black with flowers all over which are very pretty; some silver, butter knives, salt and peppers, spoons; for this winter, a couple of embroidered bedspreads; quite a lot of lace—on sale—and a very beautiful Canton shawl. The latter was a large bit of extravagance as it cost $48 reduced from $66. It is 54 inches square, black with white flowers. A really handsome object and a good investment, I think. I'm trying to stick to things that will be useful at home either as gifts or possessions.

Besides shopping, I go swimming every day in the Russian pool—an outdoors affair formed by damming up two mountain streams. It is perfectly lovely, cool and clear, and very refreshing. My usual companions are a group of youngsters, 12 to 14 years old, some from Yale and others. We have a dandy time. I was to have taken them on a hike today but it is raining for the first time this month so we've postponed it. I am developing a good tan and millions of freckles. It's hard to get a good color in a place like Changsha in the summer. One is too busy perspiring. The pool is about 1¼ mile from the home, so altogether it is good exercise.

I'm still living with Ruth Greene. She's good company and is otherwise alone, except for her servants and twin girls aged 17 months. The latter are very humorous and cute and well-behaved. Ruth says this stuff about the bond between twins is the bunk, because hers are at about the cave dweller stage of development and the older one who walks is always pulling the other's hair or snatching her toast or something. No heart at all.

I was asked the other day to help out in the hospital here, nursing an old woman who had an operation—a cholecystectomy. The hospital is full and the nurses busy and this lady rather elderly - 60 plus. Although I am on vacation away from a hospital, I couldn't really refuse so come every afternoon 2-8 p.m. It's not bad as she is in good condition, requiring little care and this type of nursing is far removed from what I do in Changsha. It's rather pleasant to sit on a breezy porch with a view over the valley with its trees and mountains at the sides, as I am right now. I think this is my last day, the third day, as she's quite all right and I don't like to be tied down to it.

If we continue to have the boat sailings to Changsha postponed, I may be able to get a job here for the winter! It would a relief in a way.

There are numerous Changsha people stranded here, including the Whipple

Huacheng:Changsha:Shanghai

family of Seattle who hoped to entertain the Blacks in Changsha when they arrive. I believe they will be in China in a few days. It is quite possible boats will resume sailing anytime and all these people will be able to return.

You have probably seen by the papers the southerners took Hankou and Hanyang and the rumor comes today they have bought off Wuchang for $60,000. They made the offer yesterday with the ultimatum that if it were not accepted and the northerners were not out of the city in 24 hours, they would shell the whole city.

I think it will ultimately go into southern hands and the Chinese realize it, so will manage a compromise rather than risk destroying the city. We read of trouble in Wahusien and wonder how it will come out. The men making trouble do not seem to be as yet acting under General Wu P`ei-fu. Probably an independent, local crowd. British are naturally much upset. We don't quite know why they are firing on passenger boats and gunboats near Hankou but they are. It's too bad not only for the shipping but because the army has made so good an impression on both foreigners and Chinese in Hankou that it seems too bad to spoil it by antagonizing people by firing which, after all, can be of no advantage to them at all. It means no mail and the only communication through the gunboat wireless. This is a great time to be living in China, history in the making and all that, yet as Ruth Greene remarked today, "One wonders why in the world we stay here where we're apparently not wanted and where earnest efforts are sometimes not appreciated."

September 22, 1926 ~ Kuling

Dear Mother,

I am still enjoying the balmy weather of Kuling, will continue to do so until the 26th when I start off for Changsha again. The weather up here has been perfect, only two days when it rained a bit and I have now a neck like a hod carrier for color. It extends down my back to the bathing suit line and my shoulders match. I've been swimming nearly every day and the water in these mountain pools is cold and stimulating. I've been twice to a lovely pool down one of the mountains, a hike of

View on Road to Kuling

about five or six miles, start at noon and go downhill over a rough rocky mountain path to a group of three pools way down mountain.

Each time, we met groups of men carrying long poles on their shoulders, like small telephone poles, toiling up slowly over the rocks, balancing the long things on their backs. I wonder how they can do it, as the poles are not lightweight. Husky men carry two lashed together like a letter A with the point in front and the cross piece for the part to rest on their shoulders. There were small boys about Burns's size who swore they were 16 or 17 years old, carrying small logs from the plains way below up to the mountaintop.

Fortunately, there is very little wood required in the stone houses we have here. We followed the coolie highway to a place where we turned off through underbrush and came upon a very rocky sort of canyon with a very mild stream flowing through it. From the sides we could see at high water it must be a powerful torrent. A natural dam of rocks in two places formed beautiful clear pools. We climbed over the boulders to the upper pool and went swimming. It was clear as crystal, every little stone perfectly seen and yet it was 10-12 feet deep in places. The sun on it made the whole thing sparkle and the cascade of water over the rocks above made it very beautiful. We swam and then had food and then swam again for the afternoon in the same pool.

In a lower one, which is fed by a high waterfall, and a still lower one fed by many little falls and a chute of racing water, we sat and slid.

I wore holes in my bathing suit and developed bruises on my bony hips where I tried going "belly flop." It was grand fun and we scrambled over rocks, got sunburned, and had a merry time altogether.

The next time, I went with Ruth Greene and a group of adults; and, the next time I took the two older Harveys and the three older Hails. The two latter are 9-year-old twins but good little hikers. I moved to the Harveys' when Ruth left last week and today I moved to the Hails' for the few days left until Sunday. I had firmly resolved not to live with Yale people, but have decided for the sake of economy and a chance to become better acquainted to risk

Harriet With The Children
At Kuling Resort Area

it. It's been pleasant and I've had a good time with all the kids.

I've done some rather extensive shopping, with the prospect of going home next summer—silver, china, a couple of grass linen bed-spreads, some lace, and a lovely Canton shawl of black embroidered in white, a thing I've wanted for a long time.

September 25, 1926 ~ Kuling

Dear Mother,

If it isn't one thing it's another in this benighted land! War in Hankou and no boats first, then that was fixed up and now it's no coolies to carry things down the mountain. We're stuck it seems as the soldiers in Kiukiang[60] take them for carriers when they return from carrying our things. I don't know what we'll do, but I'll try to get off tomorrow. I should be back at Changsha by the 30th and hate to miss it.

---

60. Kiukiang: Jiujiang, formerly transliterated Kiukiang, is a prefecture-level city located on the southern shores of the Yangtze River in northwest Jiangxi province,

Among other things I hear I'm to escort Mrs. Gilbert and her new baby back to Changsha. She left here to go home and her baby was born on the steamer in the harbor of Hankou three days earlier than expected. Isn't that wild? I don't know if they'll wait for me if I'm stuck, or go ahead.

I hear from Hankou that Mrs. Black and Antoinette arrived there en route to Changsha. I'm afraid I'll miss them if they make as short a visit as they plan.

Did you ever hear of the Whipple family who used to go to the Tabernacle Baptist Church? A husband and wife, two sons and

Paradise Pool Waterfall,
Kuling Resort Area

a daughter. They are very Fundamental and tell amazing stories about answer to prayers, etc. $2000 from a widow friend of theirs in Seattle came as an answer to prayer when they were sent to China without money enough to buy their tickets! They are very pleasant people, good fun and devoted to one another.

The elder son is about 20 or 21 and spent two years at the Los Angeles Bible Institute, mostly in music, which is all the education beyond high school he has had. His fiancée came out with the Blacks, a girl named Watson, who is a friend of Antoinette, also a Tabernacle Baptist. They're looking over the Hunan Bible Institute and then going to language school in Nanking, if they decide to stay in China; the Blacks, that is. The fiancée will stay anyhow. This is rather a hot time to visit China, with wars and turmoil and all sorts of crazy business. I'll be glad to be back in Changsha when I look at the mess in Kiukiang and Hankou, which I have to go through.

I am enclosing snapshots of your handsome daughter and the pool wherein she wallows. You can't see the layers of tan or the peeling shoulders, but they're there. It's a great life. The doctor in the hospital here, where

I cared for the old woman (age 55, by the way), invited me to spend the winter here nursing in his hospital. He's a good egg and I'd rather like to at that. I'll save the offer until I decide to come back to China!

Mrs. Pontius wrote me a letter and included a Vacation Bible School faculty picture. She gives an interesting account of a picnic at Madrona Park[61], also of Mr. Babbitt's birthday. She's a great old scout.

October 8, 1926 ~ Changsha

Dear Mother,

I found several letters waiting for me when I returned Monday. I also received a few in Kuling before I left which had been forwarded from here. It was a joy to hear about your various summer expeditions. I suppose by now the Eunices are reinstated in their little gray home in the West and all the youngsters in school.

My three weeks in Kuling were altogether most satisfactory and I'm glad I went back there again this year. It was beautiful weather the whole time, living was inexpensive and I enjoyed the Yale people although I had vowed not to even see any during vacation. Those with whom I lived—that is, the Hails and the Harveys—I do not often see, particularly now that I live on the hospital side of the campus, and am not near them during the night either.

I left Kuling as I had planned on the 26th though there had been difficulty in getting carrying coolies because the military grabbed some en route across the plains to Jiujiang and impressed them as coolies for themselves. The five older Hails walked down the mountain with me. It is about five miles mostly down rocky steps. In one place called "thousand steps," we counted 1065. As the steps were irregular in size and position, our count was not altogether accurate but it gives one an idea of the climb—descent.

We had a wait of a few hours in Jiujiang during which time I went to the Hykeses' for tea. Mrs. Hykes had gone to Shanghai to avoid possible and probable danger in the city in case the present military are the South. The foreign Concession there is a small area and has had numerous troubles in the past with looting soldiers and anti-foreign mobs. I was fortunate enough to have room allowed me in a cabin

---

61. A popular Seattle, WA city park.

with two other women. I was to sleep on a cot in the middle of the floor. However, I discovered the first officer was a man who was on the ship on which we first came up the river in '21, so we renewed our acquaintance and he let me have his cabin for the night. I felt quite exclusive, particularly as about 20 people including the Hail family had to sleep out on deck.

In Hankou, we found the Changsha boats delayed because of low water so had to wait from Monday to Friday. The weather became quite chilly and rainy and irksome. I was so desperate for something to do besides knitting and playing with the kids; I spent two days, mornings, as the secretary to the Nurses' Association, who had headquarters in the Lutheran Mission where I stayed. She was moving her office to an annex of a Chinese place so there was packing and unpacking to do, and it helped pass the time.

Meanwhile, the Gilberts were also waiting to come back here. They left Kuling about the middle of September, she being eager to get back and settled in before her baby was due to arrive in October. However, the ride down the mountain and in the auto seemed too much for her and her baby was born on the boat en route to Hankou. Fortunately, there was a doctor and nurse on board; the former, a woman of the London Mission, so she was well taken care of.

The boat being the "Tuck-wo," we call the baby "Tuck." When they reached Hankou, they were taken to the hospital where they stayed until we left on the 2nd. I was assigned to assist, offered to, in the care of both on the trip up. I slept in the upper berth, Mrs. Gilbert in the lower, and the baby in a basket on the couch. He shared the couch with an 8-year-old girl who crowded on at the last minute with her mother. The mother was a nut and suggested we let their cute little white woolly dog also sleep in our cabin. Wouldn't that have been cozy? We had to anchor at a place about three hours below here for the night and get up at 5:50 a.m. to change to a tugboat, which would be sure to get along if the river had fallen.

Deck Of MV Tuckwoy Riverboat, On Yangtze River

Fortunately, it had not fallen so we got through very hungry and tired just at noon. I chaperoned my patients to the hospital where they stayed until Saturday. Sunday morning I went over to give him, the new baby, his bath and have now officially resigned from the case except for friendly visits. I think the baby is a darling and I had a good chance to renew my enthusiasm over tiny babies. Mr. Gilbert was rather seedy himself coming up and spent large portions of the day in my upper berth. I really had three patients. The baby didn't cry at night much to the surprise of all the mamas on board who rather expected to have to apply some of their skill from experience when I, an old maid as it were, might fail to quiet him. I felt quite triumphant.

Everything is very quiet here, no fighting, no rioting, no nothing. We hear rumors of labor unions from our servants and the prospect of our doing our own work, etc., but nothing has materialized so far. The hospital coolies made demands for more pay, shorter hours, better food, and self-government and were going on strike yesterday, but they didn't. The authorities here conferred with the head military medical service to the effect if they incite our coolies to strike, it will be their own men who are patients here who would suffer. The hospital is full the whole time and the nursing situation is sad, owing to many nurses having joined the army and new nurses not intelligent enough yet to do ward work.

I'm so glad you saw the Lis. I think they are good fun. She is charming for a person who has never been out of the country before. When he was in America before, his Dad came to see him and he was so Americanized he continued talking English rather than changing to Chinese again.

Our house is settled and calm with just two of us in it. The season doesn't look very exciting in prospect, no new people here at all. However, we'll survive and probably save money.

October 12, 1926 ~ Changsha

Dear Hank,

Received a grand letter from you yesterday all about tripping over the state and Canada on pleasure bent. Sounds rather pleasant to me though my experience in motorcars to and from Kuling was not such would cause me to yearn for prolonged expeditions. The ride up in the sedan chair was more pleasant but coming down I walked the five miles with the three youngsters at whose home I had been living. They were

Harriet riding in
Sedan Chair

ages 9 (twins) and 12 and were much fun. Good little sports too and tough as dickens when it came to hiking. I took them and two more kids on a long all-afternoon jaunt one day to a mountain pool halfway down the opposite mountainside.

Harriet Modeling Swim Suit

It was a good 2-hour jaunt each way but they made it without a murmur. We spent the time there swimming or sitting on the rocks having tea, dinner being served after we got home at the usual hour of 8 p.m. The swimming was marvelous and we found a slide in a rock where a sort of cascade came down and we slid until we wore holes in the seat of our suits and then I tried a "belly flop" until I wore holes over my large hipbones. It was grand and we hopped from rock to rock like toads. I spent most of my five weeks in Kuling swimming and shall enclose a sample to prove how awesome I am in a bathing suit. I guess it would make Mack Sennett[62] sit up and take notice.

Coming home I had to wait five days in Hankou[63]—gloomy weather and nothing to do. I met quite a number of odd souls at the Lutheran Home where I stayed. After moving me from table to table at mealtime, they finally established me at a table with Navy spouses and other worldly souls. I chaperoned a 2-week old baby and mother—not to mention father, home from there. They are members of our mission and were coming home from Kuling when she got a pain and

---

62. Referring to Mack Sennett, '20s and '30s movie director known for innovation of slapstick comedy and his bathing beauties.

63. An east-central Chinese city on the Chang Jiang (Yangtze River). It is the industrial and commercial center of central China.

had the baby on the boat in the harbor of Hankou. American parents, British boat, British nurse and doctor who happened to be on board, in international waters of a Chinese river, taken to the International French hospital, where he was cared for by a German and an Austrian nurse. Then turned over to an American nurse and brought farther up Chinese waters by a British boat.

That child should be a world citizen and should enter the diplomatic corps, wouldn't you say so? He's a darling baby and I'm quite crazy about him. I occupied a stateroom with Mrs. and baby, but the husband who felt seedy spent most of each day in my bunk. Rather informal. Coming from the Yangtze River city of Kiukiang (now known as Juijiang), I slept in the First Officer's cabin, but the bunk was only big enough for one and he was on watch anyhow. He was an old China friend of mine.

The fighting in the Hankou neighborhood was nil except for occasional shots over Wuchang, the city across the river. It was besieged for over a month but shut its city gates and no one came or went. I felt positively medieval to be in a comparatively modern city like Hankou and look right over to a city closed in behind its walls and so protected from capture. As a matter of fact, the besiegers could have blown the walls down and bombed the city but they were in no hurry as they have taken all the country round about and knew all they had to do was just wait until the people, startled, opened the gates. They wanted it whole when it would be given to them. Yesterday we had word that it has finally opened, owing to the defeat of an allied commander at Jiujiang, so some of the soldiers are taken into the southern army, by just changing the insignia by opening a few safety pins, and the others are to be disarmed and sent home. No fun killing any more of them.

Here all is calm except that we have many wounded and the hospital coolies are being urged to strike, demanding higher wages, shorter hours, etc.

My friend Les Walker is still in Peking. His Dad has told him to stay a year wherever he wants to and has a small allowance with some from home to support him. On the strength of that, he's dug in for the winter and is letting the novel rest while he does a few essays and short stories as trials. I'll let you know if any of it is ever published anywhere so you can see what sort of literary genius he is. If he becomes famous and makes a million, I'll probably be sorry I didn't somehow manage to compromise him into marrying me.

I may yet have time if he's in China next summer. At present, however, it's much more convenient to have him within convenient writing distance and yet not near enough to prove a distraction. There seems to be nothing even dimly resembling a distraction here. The port is becoming a haven for young married people and the bachelors are scarce and rather sad. The British have had a bit of a damper on them by the southerners' in power here, anti-British attitude. I don't know quite what the year will bring forth.

I'm riding these days but I've had the sad luck to find that my pony is the only one of three in the stable here that is not fit to ride. I ride one of the others, however, going out with the only surviving bachelor, Southard Lenzel, who is a very nice youth but a bit callow,. "Catch 'em young," I say.

I just heard from the family they plan going east next summer and driving home with Dwight and Mrs. Dwight. That really lends a faint hope that my idea of going through Europe is not a vain dream. It is as cheap from here to England on some steamers as across the Pacific, and if I could hook a ride across the country, it would be the berries. Having absolutely no money at present, it's a wild thought to contemplate.

October 18, 1926 ~ Changsha

Dear Mother,

Regulations under which the Committee on Educational Administration expects us to operate.

REGULATIONS FOR REGISTERING A SCHOOL

(Passed at the 59th meeting of the Committee on Educational Administration and promulgated on the 18th October, 1926)

Article I. Except for special cases, schools may be established by registering with the proper educational administrative authorities. Applications for registration should be made by the administrators in the case of public schools and by the board of trustees in the case of private schools.

Primary schools and middle schools except those established by the province should file their applications and documents with the town or district bureau of education to be forwarded to the provincial bureau of education. Colleges and Professional schools except those established by the national government should file their applications and documents with the provincial bureau to be forwarded to the Committee of Educational Administration of the National Government. In forwarding these applications, the bureaus concerned must first make careful investigations and give their recommendations for reference.

The schools (or lists of schools) that have been granted registration by the provincial bureau of education must be filed through the provincial bureau with the committee of Educational Administration.

Article II. The following requirements must be met before applying for registration:

1. Finance:

a. The school must have fixed property or capital, from which the rent or income is sufficient to meet the current expenses of the year, or:

b. The school must have besides its fixed property or capital other sources of reliable income so that the current expenses of the year may be fully met.

2. Equipment: Suitable location, buildings, athletic field and other equipment for the school and for teaching purposes.

3. Faculty and staff: The faculty and staff members must have qualifications according to the standards fixed by the government. No foreigner shall be principal of a school.

Article III. In applying for registration a complete plan of the school with explanatory notes and statement of the following item must be promulgated:

a. Name of school. (Also name in foreign language, if any)

b. Kind of school.

c. System and curriculum.

d. Location.

e. List of members of faculty and staff.

f. List of students.

g. Finance and means of maintenance.

h. List of textbooks and reference books.

i. List of teaching equipment, athletic implements, apparatus, samples and models.

Article IV. The proper educational administrative authorities may annul the registration of a school, which has not been properly conducted or has shown a poor record.

Article V. A registered school may close of make changes only with the approval of the proper educational administrative authorities.

Article VI. Schools that have obtained permission to be established must apply for registration within three months of their founding.

Article VII. Students enrolled in or graduating from unregistered schools shall not receive official recognition.

Article VIII. These regulations shall be in effect from date of promulgation.

REGULATIONS FOR PRIVATE SCHOOLS

(Passed at the 59th meeting of the Committee on Educational Administration and promulgated on the 18th of October, 1926.)

Article I. All schools founded by individuals or private organizations shall be considered as "private schools." Schools established by foreigners or by religious missions are included in this category.

Article II. Private schools must be conducted under the supervision and guidance of the proper educational and administrative authorities.

Article III. The name of the private school should clearly indicate what kind of a school it is and should prefix its name by the two Chinese characters meaning "private."

Article IV. The trustees of a private school shall be elected by the founders of the school to form a board of trustees who shall be fully responsible for the development of the school. Regulations for organizing the board of trustees are promulgated separately.

Article V. The establishment of a private school of any changes to be made in such a school must be reported through its board of trustees to the proper educational administrative authorities for approval.

Article VI. In the case of closing or stopping to function of a school the board of trustees must report to the proper educational administrative authorities for approval. Its property and materials will then be jointly liquidated by the school and delegates appointed by the government.

Article VII. The principal of a private school shall be held fully responsible to the board of trustees for the execution of school affairs.

Teachers and administrative officers are appointed and dismissed by the principal.

Article VIII. No foreigner shall be the principal of a private school. Under special conditions however, foreigners may be invited to act as advisors.

Article IX. The organization, curriculum and number of hours of teaching as well as other matters pertaining to a private school must be carried out in accordance with existing government regulations.

Article X. No private school shall make religious instruction a required (compulsory) course, nor shall religious propaganda be permitted in the classroom.

Article XI. No private school shall compel students to participate in religious ceremonies, which may be carried on in the school.

Article XII. Private schools must make reports of all matters pertaining to administration and teaching at stated times according to government regulations and orders from the proper educational administrative authorities.

Article XIII. Private schools not properly managed or disobeying government orders may be dissolved (closed) by the government.

Article XIV. After the promulgation of these regulations, all private schools which have not yet been registered must apply for registration within the period specified.

Article XV. These regulations shall be in force from the date of promulgation.

REGULATION FOR ORGANIZING A BOARD OF TRUSTEES IN PRIVATE SCHOOLS.

REGULATIONS FOR ORGANIZING A BOARD OF TRUSTEES IN A PRIVATE SCHOOL (Passed at the 40th meeting of the Committee of Educational Administration and promulgated on the 18th. October, 1926.)

Article I. In a private school the board of trustees are the representatives of the founders of the school in shouldering the full responsibility of managing and developing it. In organizing the board, the founders must make a report on the following items for the approval of the proper educational administrative authority:

a. Object.

b. Name.

c. Location of executive office.

d. Regulations concerning the organization, duties and powers of the board of trustees.

e. Regulations for conducting general meetings of all founders and meeting of the board of trustees.

f. Specifications of property, endowment and other income.

Requests for forming boards of trustees for primary and middle schools should be made through the town or district bureau to the provincial bureau of education and those for colleges and professional schools should be made through the provincial bureau to the Committee on Educational Administration (central). If forwarding these petitions the bureaus concerned must first make careful investigations and give their recommendations (opinions) for reference.

The boards of trustees, which obtain their registrations at the provincial bureau of education, must also through the dais bureau, file their petitions with the committee on Educational Administration.

Article II. Within a month after the board of trustee s has been formed with the approval of the proper educational administrative authorities in accordance with the provisions laid down in Article I, a report on the following items must be presented to the same authorities for the purpose of registration. After registration has been obtained, a report to this effect should be placed on file with the local bureau where the executive office of the trustees is located:

a. Name.

b. Location of executive office.

c. Date of government approval for establishing the board.

d. Property, endowment, or other income properly itemized.

e. List of names of members of the board of trustees together with their professions, their native places and addresses.

Should there be any changes in b, d, and c, these must be reported within one week Fulfill to the proper educational administrative authorities and to the bureau of the locally where the executive office is located.

Article III. The following are the standard duties and powers of the board of trustees: (under special conditions and with the approval of the pro per educational administrative authorities there may be exceptions.

I. The financial responsibilities of the trustees toward the school.

a. Devise ways and means of raising funds.

b. Examination and approval of budget.

c. Custodianship of property.

d. Supervision of finance.

e. Other financial matters.

2. The board of trustees shall appoint a principal who alone is responsible for the direct administration of school affairs in which the trustees have no power of direct participation. The appointee must meet with the approval of the proper educational administrative authorities. In case the principal fails to discharge said duties he may be removed and another man chosen to take his place.

Article IV. The board of trustees may employ an officer to execute board affairs according to the decisions of the board of trustees.

Article V. Whenever necessary the proper educational administrative authorities may investigate into the business and financial affairs of the board of trustees of the school.

Article VI. If for any reason a school established by a board of trustees should be closed, the board must report within one week to the proper educational administrative authorities so that government representative may jointly with the school liquidate the school property. At the completion of such liquidation a report should be made to the proper educational administrative authorities.

Article VII. When a school established by a board of trustees is closed the board may with the permission of the proper educational administrative authorities, contribute the school property to some other educational enterprise.

Article VIII. If, after a school established by a board of trustees is closed there is no one to look after the school property, such property will be administered by the proper educational administrative authorities.

Article IX. Should complications arise from the assets and liabilities of the board of trustees, the matter should be settled at court.

Article X. A board of trustees can only be dissolved with the permission of the proper educational administrative authorities unless for special reasons said authorities have annulled its registration.

Article XI. Without the permission of the proper educational administrative authorities, a board of trustees cannot, of its own will close the school, which it has established.

Article XII. Within one month (50 days) of the end of the fiscal year, the board of trustees must present to the proper educational administrative authorities as well as to the educational bureau in the locality of its executive office a detailed report of the school property and on the following items:

a. Condition of school affairs.

b. Important business transacted in the year just ended.

c. An itemized statement of receipts and expenditures during the years conditions

Article XIII. Only under exceptional conditions may foreigners be admitted to the board of trustees. At all events, the Chinese should constitute the majority of the trustees and no foreigner should serve as president of the board or as chairman of the meeting of the board.

Article XIV. These regulations shall be in effect from the date of promulgation.

October 25, 1926 ~ Changsha

Dear Mother,

The letter from Father, with the reprint, came on Saturday; and, yours by Admiral Line, on Sunday, so his beat yours by a day. I think mail is coming through by train now, so there will not be the delay here or in Hankou waiting for a boat. The hopeful predictions in the British paper of Hankou that the southerners would be driven out seems to remain unfulfilled and I understand they—the Cantonese—are tearing down the Wuchang wall and are to establish their capital there, rather than in Canton. They would certainly be in a central position, with access to other large cities by rail and water. They anticipate completing the road from here to Canton, also building motor roads. It would be great from the point of view of transportation bringing Canton only days away or so, rather than having to go via Shanghai.

The address of the bank for the Fosters' money for the rugs is First National Bank of Farmington, Maine. He is Dr. John H. I hope you will send it along and still have a memo as to the amount—somewhere around $50, wasn't it? I also hope Eunice has sent the money to me in Shanghai. Exchange has been quite favorable for the past few weeks and my account is sadly depleted.

We always have expenses for coal and groceries at the school year beginning. We are using the rugs in our house and they are lovely. One large and two small of Eunice's are in the living room and the smallest one she ordered we have over a chair. It would be good for a piano bench. The round one is for you. I have it in my bedroom. My bed is on the porch so the room is more of a "boudoir," so to speak, a large chair and bureau, dressing table, etc. We are very comfortable and well settled. There is not the gang of young teachers or bachelors there was before, so the amount of cigarette ashes and dance-floor powder, which the rugs will collect, will be less.

I was glad to hear Anne Seely Gilbert will send the apples. I thought Curtiss would know better than I what brand would last longest and keep best. I have murmured it to a few other people, so I expect some—if the apples are good when they arrive— I can sell extras to with ease.

I was off duty this past weekend and had a strenuous and amusing time. Saturday afternoon I took Ruth Greene and Jess Norelius riding. My pony has been so thin, I didn't dare ride him but Ruth is so light it was all right. Jess is very heavy and bounced along like Sancho Panza[64].

After the ride, I dashed over to the Island to go rowing with Mr. Ouwerkirk who is in the APC. He has the shell, which has been in the mess for years. I've tried going before but we never arranged it. We had a fine row, sliding along between junks and sampans with all sorts of speed. As we got up to the island's end, we saw a Dr. Hartman, a German, and his wife, who signaled us to come to tea.

We had been shipping a little water and some had come over the front deck but we thought little of it until we shipped some of their wake and my feet were quite submerged. We didn't pay much attention to it, but suggested that we stage a race with death to see if we could arrive before we sank. Suddenly, we found it was coming in with a rush,

---

64. Sancho Panza, a fictional character in the novel *Don Quixote*.

we headed for shore, and just as we were arriving, down we went! We could both stand up, but the ground was so slippery that we floundered around up to our necks pulling in the boat. It was so comical that we were quite convulsed and the Hartmans were decidedly astonished to have us appear dripping wet when they'd seen us merry and dry a few moments before. Fortunately, I could wear Mrs. Hartman's clothes and Mr. Ouwerkirk could wear his, so we sat about, had dinner, and returned by launch. I suggested that we empty the shell and row back, but he wouldn't.

Sunday morning, we had another riding expedition out the Military Road, as speedy as possible, then tiffin at the Fosters' with Charlie Keller and Frank Hutchins. Charlie seems to have clanged his center of interest again. He used to spend his time having meetings and feasts here and in the city. This year he has no meetings but spends his time studying History. He hopes to get an MA next year. He has decided that one gets nowhere here if he depends on the friendship of the Chinese; that the past few years have proved that it is not to be counted on, but that he wins more confidence and respect by really knowing his subject and convincing the Chinese that he does know. There's a lot to it and it's interesting to see how Charlie changes from one thing to another, each occupying the center of his attention while it lasts.

I am now in the choir's alto section, rehearsals on Thursday. It's good fun for a change. We sang "Sing Alleluia Forth" yesterday. Shades of Pilgrim!

What a surprise is Charlotte's matrimonial prospect. I should think it would make the family a bit ill, especially Aunt Carrie who was always the enthusiastic Zionist. I'll promise not to marry a Jew or a Dane, but how about a Chinese or a South American? We aim to please.

We're having decent fall weather now after three weeks of cold and rain. Our dispositions improve accordingly.

Please give my best regards to Frank. I mean to write a special letter to him one of these days. I wish there were more of his kind in his native land. He could teach them dependability and industry, especially now that we're getting a few Communist doctrines taught to them.

October 28, 1926 ~ Changsha

Dear Mother,

I am mailing today a small package of x-stitch and a few Mandarin squares. I got 20% off on the usual price of x-stitch as a Mission member. My idea is that you may keep as many pieces as you could use for Christmas presents. They are the sorts of gifts they seem to like to buy for small presents. I wrote Elizabeth Henry that I'd send these things and for her to show them to the library girls who seemed to like some I had last year. Will you let her know, or send them to her? I would suggest changing the prices as listed, only in gold instead of Mex. At present exchange it will be more than twice the cost. However, you might alter some yourself if you think they are too much or too little. Experience tells me not to charge too much. What you don't get rid of, park in my camphor chest, please, or keep for yourself or Eunice.

The Mandarin squares I think are particularly fine. Have you sent a package to South America? If not, will you include one for Alice from me? Thanks. I think any of them would be lovely in a tray or even framed in a picture. I bought them from Dwight's old friend Chow who has some very nice things now, not all ancient, smelly clothes. If you make anything on it, or if Elizabeth sells any (commission 50%), just credit me or pay for the apples with it. The stuff cost me $55.08 Mex, which is about $17 gold. If you pay $7 or so duty and can sell it, there is a possibility of $8 or $10 to make. What a hope. Anyhow, do as you like about it. I'll be sending a Christmas package later.

October 31, 1926 ~ Changsha

Dear Hank,

Yes, it's me again. I'm letting you know that I've made good my threat about sending some dinky pieces of x-stitch—sent to my mother—in case you care about showing some to the library girls who seemed to like some I had last year. Please pocket 50%—it may be all of $1.59. Anyhow, that would be enough to buy a bath salt for someone, ain't it.

This old boss ain't what she used be. I've joined the Prince of Wales club by breaking a collarbone—thrown from my horse. Sounds better than saying I fell. In fact, I was riding by myself, the pony slipped in the mud and fell, rubbing his nose in the dirt and I went over her head in a dive which landed me on my right shoulder, thereby fracturing the clavicle.

Unfortunately, I had poor taste to do it when out by myself, no gallant gentleman to rescue me, or there to sympathize—just poor technique, that's all. Phil Greene, MD, put me in a cast about the shoulders and I shed bits of plaster all along the way.

The night after I fell, I went out to dinner to the very stylish "Friday Club." I came home alone, meeting the remaining bachelor, Southard Lenzel, en route. He came in and we chattered a while till we both got sleepy so he started home. I suddenly remembered I couldn't get out of my clothes alone, my dress being a high-collared sleeveless middy blouse sort of thing over a lace under-slip. Therefore, it must be either he or the coolie, so I begged him to kindly assist, which he did, very politely but very much embarrassed. Rather unique request to make of one's escort.

Did I tell you about going rowing in a shell here—a two-man, double-oared racing boat with a Dutchman named Ouwerkirk of the APC (Asiatic Petroleum Company.) We had a grand time until we shipped so much water we submerged just off shore and both went dripping into the house of some of his German friends. It was most amusing, especially in the clothes they lent us!

Otherwise, life is calm. Les Walker is to be in Peking all winter. I'd be curious to have him meet Marjorie McKillop. They might hit it off well. There's no one about here interesting matrimonially unless it is Charlie Keller who is, I suppose, a bachelor again. He's a dear but erratic as the deuce.

November 4, 1926 ~ Changsha

Dear Mother,

Things move on here much the same with a few interesting exceptions. One I might mention has direct bearing on my "scrawly" handwriting, worse than usual, and that is that my shoulders are all done up in a plaster cast because I was thrown from my pony like the Prince of Wales and fractured my right clavicle. I think Burns and Betty and I could now form an exclusive society. The most annoying part, romantically speaking, is that I was alone, and had no one to rescue me or to sympathize at the time.

I've had many expressions of sorrow since, particularly since I have this messy, crumbling lot of plaster. That is Phil Greene's method of splinting such a break. In fact, the bone was in good position according to the x-ray so it was just a matter of keeping it so, rather than reducing a deformity. I trust it has stayed so. It was a week ago tonight and Phil thought he'd take it off and apply some other sort of splint as we had the bad luck to a very poor lot of plaster. It hasn't bothered me to speak of except in dressing, eating and sleeping, and makes my writing a bit cramped. After all, its not important and small people like Betty have it without knowing it.

Another annoyance is that it temporarily keeps me from riding and the weather is quite ideal at present. I'm hoping for it to continue so. The trouble last week was we were riding rapidly homeward and rounding a corner. The pony' front feet slipped and she fell on her nose, I going over her head landing on my right shoulder and rolling onto my back. At that moment, the pony recovered her balance and stepped gently on my pelvis, so to speak.

November 8, 1926 ~ Changsha

Dear Mother,

Just as I was writing this, I had a call and have not had an opportunity to finish. The night I wrote the above, Phil removed my cast but it was so uncomfortable and the callous wasn't hard enough so on Saturday he did me up again in an adhesive Velpeau bandage[65] minus the one that comes from the elbow across the front to the shoulder. That's done with a sling. It's quite comfortable and we're all happy again. In another week I ought to be solid enough to come out of it entirely.

Letters came from home a few days ago. It was fine to hear from you, including my two brothers, a surprise from which I am just now beginning to recover. I shall surprise them in turn by answering promptly and then it will be their turn again. As for the newspaper clipping from the *Times*, they seem to have got it straight, which is the main consideration.

---

65. Many varieties of swaddling bandages for injuries of the shoulder are in use and are called Velpeau bandages.

They didn't say anything about wanting a regular correspondent out here at 8¢ a word, did they? I might be so bashful as to say there are interesting things happening in the city and agitations, which are history making.

For instance, our servants are just now being organized into labor unions. We received notices from the International Organization of Workers that there would be a servants' meeting Sunday at 2 o'clock and they expected the servants to have vacation for an hour. That in China may mean anything from 2 to 4 hours. We were not home for tiffin so don't know how long they stayed. They are expecting to present demands, just as the students in various schools have done and are doing. I suppose the first will be for increased wages, a pension fund, a system of increasing their wages, and sick benefits. The part that seems to

Harriet as China Correspondent

Daily Times

NDAY, OCTOBER 11, 1926.

MISS HARRIET H. SMITH of Seattle, who is with the Hunan-Yale Hospital, Changsha, China.

—Photo by Grady Studio.

SEATTLE GIRL WRITES OF WAR

Miss Harriet Smith Has Many Experiences in Midst of Chinese Strife.

EVENTS that no doubt will fill Chinese history books for centuries to come, are everyday experiences to Miss Harriet H. Smith, daughter of Dr. and Mrs. C. A. Smith, 1305 E. Mercer St., and now assistant superintendent of Hunan-Yale Hospital or Yali, at Changsha, China.

In recent letters to her parents, Miss Smith has described, in vivid detail, the march of the Southern Army toward Hankow, scenes in Hankow as the Southern Chinese approached it, and has given interesting sidelights on some of the leading figures on the Chinese political stage.

Marshal Chiang Kai Shik, head of the Southern Army and successor to Sun Yat Sen, is the "Silent Cal" of China, she implies in relating an incident that occurred when he sent for the hospital dentist to examine his teeth.

Marshal Chiang Likes Simplicity.

"The doctor and his assistant went off in grand style, with all their instruments and equipment," the letter says. "While they waited for him to appear they were served with coffee and tea, and allowed to sit in a very hot room. People kept coming in and going out, until finally one man in shirt sleeves and suspenders, came in and shook hands with them in a business-like way. Dr. Green beamed at him and asked 'And what is the gentleman's name?' The man replied 'Chiang,' just like that. It makes a lovely story, considering the style of Chinese expression, and rates with some of the Coolidge stories. At least, Marshal Chiang does not surround himself with pomp and ceremony."

En route from Changsha to Hankow in September, Miss Smith was in the fighting zone.

"We saw no signs of the Southern Army until we were a few hours from Hankow. A few shots were fired at us there, none of which came nearer than a quarter of a mile, according to the captain. That was quite near enough.

Chinese Leave Hankow.

"In Hankow there was a prevailing air of expectancy. The Chinese were hurrying through the streets, bag and baggage, by foot and by rickshaw, taking their families and possessions to safety in the foreign concessions. The servants' quarters in all the houses in the concessions were filled with people, and behind all their gates were rows of Chinese faces. At any time during the day one could hear the constant scurry of feet through the streets, a regular Pied Piper of Hamlin exodus from the Chinese city.

"In the morning there was heavy firing in Wuchang and we could impress our cook the most is what will be the really annoying part of it, which is that we will not he able to fire a servant without the permission and union sanction, and they may fire a servant of whom they do not approve whether we want to retain him or not.

In case we would not agree, they would boycott us and boycott any others with whom we would try to board. It may not be as bad as that, and may take a long time to get into operation and the South may be driven back to Canton before it goes into effect, if one could believe the British papers.

I must say I would be ashamed to think I could not cook and keep house perfectly well without any domestics, but there is the difficult matter of shopping. The servants go out into the street about 6 a.m. and buy directly from the farmers who bring in their produce early in the morning. We were economical in the matter of tinned goods this fall, thinking we would use more fresh foods. It is cheaper but may fool us in the end. We shall see.

The pathetic part of it is that many servants haven't any idea what it is all about, many of them only a foggy idea, and many of them have no inclination to do any different from what they are now doing. I don't know whether the union would support them if they walk out, or what would happen. The Amahs[66] seem particularly upset as they have no "jining" instincts and are afraid they will lose their jobs and have to desert their mistresses and small charges. It is quite sad to hear them go on.

We had a small taste of it last week. One afternoon I was up on one ward when a coolie from another ward came and said, "Go down" to the other coolies. They all dropped their work and departed. One murmured "back soon" but others said nothing. I had an idea they were holding a meeting somewhere, which was the case. It was about their wages. They had presented 12 demands to the hospital several weeks ago and they had been settled in that some of them received a 50¢ a month increase, and others were to be increased $1 at the month end, and those others an additional 50¢ a month increased $1 to make them all equal. That was the way the treasurer understood it. The 50¢

---

66. A woman employed as a children's nurse, domestic servant, office cleaner, or attendant.

men were demanding a dollar raise just like the others, in addition to the former increase.

They were all gone from the wards for about 2 hours. Just before that time was up it was the hour for patients to have their evening meal. We sent some new probationers down to bring it up, but they were afraid the coolies would hit them, so I took over the job of escorting other foreign nurses and dished out the food down in the kitchen. The old Head Cook was aghast, fearing for his own skin, and amazed to condescend to do that sort of work. Fortunately, the probationers took it as sort of a lark so we had no trouble with them. Just as we had the food all up on the wards, the coolies came back and it was their turn to register surprise that the food could have come without their help. They have been perfectly quiet since.

Their row was settled in an amusing way. It seems Dr. Yen is playing around with the new government and all their pals, so on that particular day he's at some sort of feast with them. Then word came the coolies had gone off. He was sitting next to the labor union head, who sent word they were to behave and go back to work. Evidently, they could not have their good time interrupted with any such foolishness.

The new Russian Consul has moved into the house where the nurses lived during the spring and summer, the Extraterritorial Palace. I don't know whom he "consuls," the Soviet I suppose. He is a quiet little person and Dr. Houston, who had been taking care of the Russian's wife, says they are pleasant people.

Yesterday was the anniversary "Russian Revolution," or founding of the Soviet Republic, I guess. There was a huge parade all afternoon, taking about 3 hours to pass. They had to all come out here to honor the Russian by passing through his house and grounds, I understand. The farmers' union led, and then came workers, servants, and finally students. I don't know how they liked being relegated to the last ranks. Yet there are those who say Russia is not interested in the Kuomintang. We all wondered if they would do the same to the British on Empire Day, to the French on Bastille Day, and to us on the 4th of July. Yes, I think so!

Everything they say and do has an anti-British note to it. They are certainly hot against them. It is all so unreasonable and hysterical from the point of view of the mass of people who haven't a vague idea what a "Britisher" is, or why they should oppose them. The stores are full of British goods and many clothes are made of it and worn by the very ones who cry, "Kill the English." It is too bad to school a naturally peaceful and friendly nation into lessons of hatred and prejudice.

I heard one schoolteacher say she was going to find out from history what day it was Sun Yat-sen was saved by the British from being killed by the Manchus when he was in London preaching against the Manchus, and then she is going to make a speech about it. It would be a good idea but the sad part of it would be the students wouldn't believe her, though she has been 20 years in China spending all those years for the schoolgirls' benefit.

That is the whole pathetic business it seems; people like the Gottenbergs miserable and unhappy because the people on the streets shout insults at them; and, to have some of their faithful old workers turn against them and leave them in the lurch with no support or thanks. I wonder how much of that side of it you get at home.

If returning missionaries, particularly those from Kwantung,[67] speak their real minds about it, I suppose you have heard some sad stories of disillusionment and disappointment. I had dinner last evening with a Norwegian, Mr. Kiaer, who is in the YMCA here. He says they are not allowed to advertise in the newspapers or send out any notices or to have any printing done and this is the time for their membership drive. I suppose it is the Christian part that gives them an excuse to boycott it, and the fact that one secretary is of British parentage, and birth.

The YMCA here has been unique for years in that it was entirely supported by local gifts from the Chinese themselves and they have just put up a fine new building, beautifully equipped. They were counting on the present membership drive to finish meeting their debt and to pay the salaries of the Chinese secretaries, some of whom have had no pay for 5 months. Now this Communist influence has come along, accusing the building of being too fine for the common people, that it is a tool of Imperialism and all that sort of thing printed in the daily paper.

---

67. Kwantung: A former coastal territory of northeast China in southern Manchuria. Leased to Russia in 1898, controlled by Japan from 1905 to 1945, and leased to Russia again from 1945 until 1955, when it was returned to China.

I suppose they really hope to finish it off as a YMCA organization by these means and then use the building and plant as headquarters for an organization of their own. It is a gloomy prospect for the men, both Chinese and foreign, to see their efforts of years being taken away from under their very noses. I wonder what our friend, the Reverend Sydney Strong,[68] would say to it all, as it is a direct reflection of dear Moscow, of course.

One annoying part is there are so many individuals we have met at the hospital as patients who are so pleasant and gentlemanly. I think they are quite apart from the labor side, being in the army. There is one here now who reminds me of father's friend, the Yale man. His name is Yao and he had his leg shot and then amputated here. He was for 17 years in Russia until five years ago and has been back in his native land long enough to appreciate the benefits of any foreign country. He says China is really a terrible place compared with any European country or America and his advice to me is to go back and enjoy myself again. That is the opinion of most students who have been in foreign countries. I think it is harder for them to readjust to life in their own country again than for us to come here and live comfortably. This Kuomintang movement has appealed to them as seeming to be the real hope for a unified country and there are many of them in it.

Did I tell you I have been given half of the nursing administration, known as Superintendent of Nurses? That doesn't mean much except I have charge of the nurses when they are on duty in the hospital, and have the graduates under my direct charge. Also I am in charge of affairs connected with the hospital and the nurses, and am to meet the doctors.

Miss Gage continues to direct the school and is known as Dean of the Nursing School. She had thought of turning over part of the administration before. I remember hearing about it when I was here before, but it had never been done. She has been like a dragon to the doctors ever since she came back and it was partly for this they were restless to have me come back. Dr. Yen is a slick old egg if there ever

68. Reverend Sydney Strong, was a pacifist Congregationalist minister from Seattle, WA, and practitioner of the social gospel and, also, active with the Industrial Workers of the World (I.W.W.). Read more of the Reverend and his daughter, Anna Louise Strong, and their involvement with the US Communist Revolution movement. http://www.lib.washington.edu/specialcoll/findaids/docs/papersrecords/StrongAnnaLouise1309_1444.xml

was one. Dr. Houston is the one who talked to me about it first and was all for throwing Miss Gage out by the scruff of her neck and telling her to stay there, but it seemed a bit rough. She for some reason has nothing good to say of him and it was next to impossible to get anything satisfactory done between the medical and nursing services. I am to be sort of a buffer, or a tool in the hands of the medics! However, if it makes them any happier I am willing to do what I can for the cause. I have written to Miss Hall asking her to send me standard hospital outlines for keeping nurses' accounts and arranging duties and all that, as it is done in the best families (hospitals) at home. I would like to get in operation soon.

Our latest addition is a German doctor named Mauck, who was in a government medical school in Wuchang, which has been disorganized. He was in Petrograd and chummed about and played duets with Rachmaninoff. We've had no such wonderful pianist here, ever; it's a treat to hear him play

November 19, 1926 ~ Changsha

Dear Mother,

I am writing again to you though I haven't the slightest idea when the mail will leave. These "crazy birds" around here have been doing the strike business so the trains have stopped and the river is too low for the boats. We've had no outside word for about a week, as there was a post office strike there the week before. There seems to be some question whether or not it is over yet. I think there was a general strike in Hankou—that's what I mean by "there"—but of course we have not been able to hear if it is over yet.

I can't say I blame the railroad people for striking, as they have not been paid for several months. They have had to carry troops and all that and have had no pay for it, and no prospect of any. Here we have had no servants' strikes, and the students have behaved all right since some sort of fancy arbitration settled them. It is interesting to see how it all works out. There is no money to pay the railroad and all that and yet there is enough to keep a labor organization going and, too, offer strikers 60¢ a day, as I am told, with 20¢ of it coming from our Soviet Consul down the street from us.

Dr. Houston says the amount the Soviet Government appropriates for propaganda is much less than appropriated by foreign firms such as Standard Oil and a great deal less than the missionary boards. Still they seem to be able to do considerable damage with their propaganda budget. We have great fun figuring out what we will do if the servants strike and all that, but none of us really knows what would happen. There are those who will scab even in China. I think and believe we could develop some vegetable bootleggers from across the fence.

However, I think that would hardly be a pleasant way to live and not being one of those who believe in cramming down their throats what the Chinese, for the time being, seem not to want. I would rather join the ranks of those who would go home for a vacation.

I have invited the whole Mission to our house in Seattle for Christmas in case we get that far by then. That will mean about 60 people, but I guess we could stand it. What do you say? Just the same, there is a small chance that it may seem best to send us home some time this year. There are those who advocate closing the college at China at New Year's time when the kids are home for vacation. The trouble with closing it in the middle of a term or having the kids go on strike is they camp on the premises and won't get out.

I think everyone believes things will be straightened out in a few years, or perhaps months, and they wonder whether it wouldn't be better to anticipate it by a few weeks and thereby save time and money and peoples' spirits.

Last week, the school had a two-day holiday for Sun Yat-sen's birthday and this week the Students' Union declared a day and a half holiday for remembering the affair at Wanhsien, which happened about 2 months ago. They all have to go out and parade or send representatives, but those chosen wouldn't go and leave the others to enjoy a warm and quiet holiday while they had to march on the streets, so they all went.

I have a hunch that if the Communists want to drive the foreigners to close their schools, they will see the time is all broken into this way and the courses upset so that it will not seem worthwhile to try to keep up with the work. That would seem the consistent thing to do. I don't know what the leaders have in mind to do after they close foreign and mission schools. That is, whether they will hope to appropriate the property or open rival schools or what. We shall probably find out! They have persuaded many students in mission schools to demand they do not teach Bible anymore, even in the primary schools, some Christian teachers being leaders in the agitations.

The Powells' adopted Chinese children are all upset because their teachers are trying to get them and all the other primary school students to organize. That shows how absolutely ridiculous it becomes at times. At the same time, it has served to discourage and depress the school head, who has been in China for years. So it goes.

We are very peaceful and quiet here at the hospital at present. All goes on as usual, and with an oily guy like Dr. Yen at the helm we shall probably be at least diplomatically guided through any storm that may develop. Our soldiers are gradually leaving, but we are still full, and I am busy with my new duties as well as the former ones.

Our dog is very cute. We call him Skippy—short for "Skip the gutter." Not bad!

There really is no other news or anything of interest. I'll be glad to hear from you when and if there is mail. Our chrysanthemums are beautiful this year, just like hothouse ones at home. I am finding out the very best and proper way to cultivate them and shall suggest it as a treatment for those of ours at home.

December 1, 1926 ~ Changsha

Documents from the Hunan Bureau of Education and The 24th Special Group of the Changsha of the Kuomingtang
The following two documents are very telling of attitudes and policies the hospital and school had to contend with.

December 1, 1926

Hunan Bureau of Education

Order Number 11 "Chao":

For College of Yale in China (private)

The following order has been received from the Committee of Educational administration of the People's Government (Canton):

"In recent years, schools established by private individuals or private organizations have often been conducted not in accordance with government regulations and rarely by truly responsible persons. In particular few of the schools established by foreigners and by religious missions have reported and registered according to regulations. This is quite contrary to our educational laws. Unless regulations are clearly laid down we are not able to show the standard requirements and expect these to be followed or fulfilled. We have now specifically made the following sets of regulations for the particular purpose of regulating the schools:

a. Regulations for private schools.

b. Regulations for establishing board of trustees in a private school.

c. Regulations for registering a school.

Besides submitting these regulations to the government and promulgating them, we are sending you a copy of these regulations with the expectation that all private schools under your jurisdiction will conduct themselves in obedience to these regulations. The whole procedure (for registration) must be completed before April 1, 1927. It is expected that in the mean time reports will be made concerning the progress of the work."

In accordance with the above order we are promulgating the regulations and we expect that the principal of your school will act accordingly. This is very important.

Please find enclosed a booklet containing the regulations for private schools, for boards of trustees and for registration.

Signed and stamped with official seal,
Chow Ngo Sen
Provincial Commissioner of Education for Hunan Province.

THE 24TH SPECIAL GROUP OF THE CHANGSHA OF THE KUOMINGTANG

DECLARATION OF ITS FOUNDING DISTRICT

We, the special bureau, the 24th of the District of Changsha of the Kuo Ming Tang have formed our organization today. From three or four persons to over a hundred persons our society can make such founding not only on the exertions of our few old comrades, but also on the fact that the policy and principles of our party are suitable and needed by the vast majority of our people. Otherwise the efforts of the few will not bring any results. Look at Nationalist Party! They have not failed to spread propaganda. But what is the result? The intelligent ones have already thrown it out of their mouth. And those who are progressive in their thinking, though fooled for a time, have retired from such a group, hand in hand and decided to enter our party. Therefore we can say as a certainty that the principles and the policies of our party under the present condition are more complete than those of any other party. In other words, in order to emancipate the mass of our Chinese people under the present conditions, there is no other way except through the Revolution of the citizens gained by our party.

Very good. Our Divisional Bureau is established. Of course we always will receive guidance from our superior party organizations. From now on our activities in the revolutionary movements of our citizens will and we will not be based upon the principles and policies of our party and not be behind others in participating in these activities be guided and led with heat and violence. Our comrades in this Division come from Hsiang-Ya Medical School, Hsiang-Yali Hospital and Yali. Our environment is much worse than that of any other group of our comrades. We do not only receive the oppression of imperialism and militarism and that of local rascals and bad gentry which our comrades elsewhere receive, but we are given a saturated intoxication from the invasion of foreign culture and we are attacked by the Nationalist Party and are under the intrigues of imperialists and foreign slaves. Therefore our comrades in this special district have to do the things that our comrades elsewhere are doing, and besides must press right away for a solution of the questions facing our particular group, questions which are described separately below:

Yali College of Yale-in-China

Our one policy toward foreign nations is to abolish the unequal treaties between China and other organizations. Since the missionary schools are the products of unequal treaties, therefore they are the objects of our attack. Now we know that which comes with unequal treaties must also be destroyed at the same time the unequal treaties are destroyed. So that now our activity will be directed toward the end that these unequal treaties will never have any effect. But since the Mission Schools have so much influence in our Chinese society and since the students are all Chinese we cannot ignore them. We want to try our best to carry out the following things:

a. To help to the utmost the Revolutionary Student Union! To sympathize with the student union of our party. To increase the strength so the authorities of Yali will not oppress that it.

b. Those teachers and staff officers who do not deserve their office shall without any ceremony request to come down from their platform. At Yali among the teachers whether American or Chinese it is true there are a good many deserving ones. But those who do not know what they are to do are not few in number. This latter class of teachers and staff members often borrow pompous dignity of American Imperialism to threaten, students. For example: If they cannot answer the question asked by the students they will say these are "foolish questions". If the students ask any further then they are punished for insulting superiors or even expelled from school. Their real ability is below that of young students. Let us ask a fair question. Should this kind of teachers be allowed to remain? In the future, if similar incidents happen, honestly and without ceremony we will ask them to pack up quickly.

Hsiang-Ya Medical School:

Chinese and Americans originally jointly managed this school. At the expiration of the agreement last year, American control was withdrawn so that in name the school is a pure Chinese school. In practice, the power of the Americans is still very great. Among the teachers it is true there are many who are rather well educated. There are also many who are rice pots. Take for instance, the two American doctors in Pathology and X-ray. They have absolutely no knowledge concerning their two branches of learning. If they should love themselves, or if the Americans should have less power in this school than they actually have, these people would have resigned or been forced to resign; but they have not only failed to resign or been forced to do so by the school authorities, but they have even put on an unduly haughty air. Why should we want these rice pots here? We hope they will exert themselves to improve their knowledge and reform their attitude; otherwise should any un-ceremonial affair occur, the responsibility will not be ours.

The darkest curtain in the Mission Schools is the way the faculty promotes students or demotes them. That is based entirely upon their personal feelings and not at all upon any standards or regulations. This last summer in the Hsiang-Ya Medical School there was one Mr. Tsang. Although his record was not 100% good, compared with several of his classmates who were not demoted, his record was better than theirs. Simply because he was not well versed in flattering so the t he could please one or two teachers, without any reason he was demoted. Now, our brethren, what sort of business is this? Why should a man be trodden under foot like this? And that with our reason. Very good. Let by-gones be by-gones. But what is coming must be regulated. In the future if such a thing occurs we shall severely interfere.

Hsiang-Ya Hospital

a. Laborers.

The laborers are a great portion of the sufferers in our nation.

At the same time they are the most important soldiers in our revolutionary army. This cannot be denied by anyone. In order to accelerate the revolutionary movement and in order to revolutionize the kind of revolution brought about in the past by the classes of property owners and capitalists, our party extends to them extraordinary help so that their revolution will develop. During the past few years our party has got more results from the laboring classes than from any other classes. This is an evidence of the clarity of vision of our Tsung Li. In the direction of developing labor movements. But when goodness rises one foot the evil spirit rises ten The time for the development of labor movements is also the period of anti-revolutionaries to intensify their oppression. Under the militarist regime these anti-revolutionaries openly and boldly oppress laborers. Under the revolution-ary government these men secretly plot to destroy the labor unions As to these anti-revolutionaries, the labor organizations should, of course, resist them and destroy them. But our party, which is the representative before the people, should take positive measures to wipe out these people and dig the hospital in any unreasonable way, the comrades of our party will deal with them, cost what it may!

b. Nurses.

The Hunan-Yale Nursing School ever since it's founding has been controlled entirely by Americans. Thus the actions of the students are supervised by these women. If anyone should oppose their foolish policies or express dissatisfaction with their intoxicating medicine - their Christianity - in words or actions, he or she is immediately expelled. The foreigners have raised up a group of running dogs among the students who will accept their orders in order to strengthen their own positions. Consequently these innocent students are ordinarily so scared that they do not dare to move or talk. The whole day they will only respect the foreigner and thank God. This kind of contempt darkens the sky and the sun. Who can bear it? If we do not emancipate them from this world of darkness what is the use of talking about revolution? From now on, we are not going to allow these foreign nurses who eat but do not labor, to act as they please. And we are going to exert to our utmost to succor these innocent men and women nurses who are now being oppressed in the 18th Hell.

Concerning the three above organizations, Hospital, Medical School and Yali, it is impossible to completely expose their illegal actions. There are many things to be reorganized. We shall mention in passing one or two examples. We hope those who oppress and those who are against the revolution will sincerely repent their former sins and stop being running dogs and anti-revolutionists.

Lastly we have decided to drive away the foreign slave, H.C.Tsao who has been so strongly entrenched in Hsiang-Ya. From this Province the District Bureau of the Kuomintang party has also decided to drive him away. The resolution was published in the Dec. 1st. issue of the Hunan Ming Bao under the heading, "Record of the District Executive Committee Meeting. "We have done so absolutely without any personal grudge against this person. It was because of thx his words and actions, which showed the deep color of anti-revolution. We thought in laying aside personal feelings, in insisting upon his immediate expulsion we would not shake the foundations of the hospital. The hospital of the Chinese people. Of course when the rabbit dies the fox is grieved. Those who are related to him perhaps may feel the fright of cold teeth from which the lips have been drawn back. That is true. Our party will end; be ceremonious in wiping out the anti-revolutionary group. But if we cannot prove to quite the same extent as in the case of the foreign slave Tsao, their anti-revolutionary actions, and if they should be sincerely penitent over their former wrongs and not oppose our party, then our party will be willing to widen its bosom and give to such a new road. Lastly we have a few words for the foreigners who are present connected with the three organizations. The object of our party is to destroy imperialism and abolish unequal treaties. Our attitude toward the foreigners as long as these do not smell stinky of politics and come to China as spies to disturb the peace of our nation, as long as they do not talk ill and look down upon our party we shall not fail to treat them as equals. We shall be particularly willing to treat as honored guests our employed teachers and professional advisors. The mission schools and other institutions will naturally be destroyed when unequal treaties are destroyed en bloc. At such a time if foreigners suitable we shall heartily welcome them. On the other hand if they depend upon the adulterous pomp and power of imperialism to disturb peace among us and to oppress the people, then without any ceremony we shall deal severely with them. We hope from this declaration all people will recognize the true principles of our party and extend to each other a lifting hand so that the peop1e's revolution will succeed in the near future. Now we shall shout very loudly:

Down with Imperialism, Down with Militarism! Down with Commodore Classes! Down with Foreign Slaves! Down with all the Antirevolutionaries.

The people must quickly join our party and stand behind the people's government.

December 1, 1926 ~ Changsha

Dear Mother,

I have been expending a few hours of labor and a few minces in cash to send off Christmas letters to various people, and have gone so far as to send a few packages also. The one to you is rather meager but it is intended to remind those at home I have not forgotten them and to assure you all I shall try to do better next summer in the remembrance line. I figure if this mail goes through, as it should on Christmas Day. I guess it will arrive without me after all, so will carry best wishes to you all as though I were there to say "Best Wishes" to you all as though I were there to say so myself.

We had what seemed almost like Christmas a few days ago when a very long-delayed mail arrived. I had not heard from home since the first of November and it was four weeks until this mail finally came. We had begun to think the bandit-soldiers who robbed a boat below here a few miles had made off with the mail, as well as with the Captain who, by the way, was intact but minus about $1200.

It is possible they may have had something to do with the delay and it's also possible they made off with some mail permanently, but complaints have ceased now that we have received some news of the great outside world. Things seem to be moving along pleasantly with you at home, except for the excitement Eunice writes in connection to President Suzzallo[69]. Is there any talk of his replacing our popular Governor? It all sounds very thrilling. However, we are so callous on the subject of meetings and protests and all sorts of things, that we pay no attention to anything like that anymore.

This is history that is going on all around us for sure, and if the Chinese temperament were anything like the Russians, I could understand all about the revolution in Russia. However, the Chinese, being a naturally calm and peaceful people, do not rise or sink to the levels of their friends in the West.

I think I have written you regarding the Yali student demands. The Middle School students presented them, and most were settled temporarily all right. The next outfit after the hospital coolies, who demanded and received a raise, was our servants. They had a meeting several weeks ago and an informal statement of their demands was passed to Mr. Hail from his boy.

The ensuing cussing and discussing can hardly be imagined by anyone who has not lived on the Yale campus at Changsha. Suffice it to say the sessions were lengthy and wordy at least, and the conclusion

---

69. Henry Suzzallo was president of the University of Washington until he stepped down in 1926.

was we give each servant a raise of $3 a month. That does not seem like much considering servants' wages at home, but it does mean quite a lot to some families who hand out over 10% of their monthly salary in wages. We now pay $40 a month for three as opposed to the former $50 for four when I was in China before.

The whole population has gone wild on the subject of Unions and holding meetings and having parades. Every day there is a parade of some sort, the other morning one being announced by a blast of trumpets and a ruffle of drums proved to be the fishermen's union. It included those who catch and sell and dry or in any way have anything to do with fish. There is also a union of women and girls who pick over and sort pig bristles for brushes, etc.

Over at Dr. Houston's house the other night, one intern was apologizing for not having come to dinner, but he said he was helping to organize a union. Mrs. Houston spoke up and said that was the one she wanted to join, that anything he started would suit her perfectly. I thought he was going to pass out with amusement and embarrassment, and could understand why when I heard the union was one for wet nurses. It seems they want to be assured of an income from the child's family after the child has grown. They insist the child's health and well being is due to them rather than to the mothers, which is the case in many families where the mother has practically nothing to do with the child at all.

Then Hilda Yen told of another union, that of concubines. They want equal rights with the wives, though as Hilda says, in most cases they are better off than the wives because they are usually the man's choice rather than having it arranged by his family, and they are the ones who go out in society with him and their children have the same status as the number one wife's children. It is so ridiculous one wonders where it will end.

Some predict it will end soon, the substantial people will tire of all the parading business and when the parades are a bit weary then they will step in and reorganize things back to normal level again. I think it is not as easy as all that. It has gone too far to be so easily readjusted. All the working people have struck for, or are receiving higher pay, which means the cost of things is going up also. They have been assured, poor things, that food and clothes will not go up in price, but I think their informers are the same ones who are taking their $5 extra pay for this month as union dues. It is a bit sickening but that is the way it is, according to our boy who is a simple soul and not one to romance on the subject.

According to the papers, Hankou is getting it in the neck worse than we. There they have the Concessions, of course, so the foreigners are neatly concentrated in one place, and easier to handle in the way of pickets and all. I don't know how the foreign firms are getting along but here they have very little business, especially the British. There is nothing violent. They are using more subtle means and really more effective ones. The Soviet Consul down here must be a busy man. Dr. Houston has told me the money assigned by the Soviet for propaganda in China is less than appropriated by some business firms, like Standard Oil, and a good deal less than spent by the Missions, and yet how efficiently it has been used! It fairly makes one's hair stand on end.

As for our position here, for some reason or other they have picked on Mr. Tsao, our hospital manager, for the subject of criticism in the papers, and it has reached such a point the medical students demanded he be sent away. This was the result of orders from headquarters, undoubtedly, and yet it has meant he has left the hospital.

The first idea was that he would be sent by Dr. Yen to visit different provinces to raise money. A neat way of putting it, but now I understand he will hang around and see what is decided at the hospital board meeting tomorrow, and then act. They are to reorganize the Hsiang-Ya board that was changed to be one with Chinese majority last year to rate a donation from the Rockefeller Fund. Now most of the old goats on it are out of sight and out of the province.

They were all Chao Hung Ti people and not mentioned now that the Kuomintang is here. If the new members are to be Kuomintang members, as I suppose they are, I don't know what that will mean next, or who they will decide should be the next to go. I rather suspect it might be Dr. Yen. Keep this dope under the well-known hat, please, until we see what happens. This is just advance speculation. Anyhow I understand that Dr. Yen says that if Mr. Tsao is forced to go, he will go also. It looks a bit that way, as Hilda is giving away her horse, and they are disposing of their beloved dogs. In that case, with neither of them here, and no foreigner like Dr. Hume—not that his word would count for much now—we wonder what the future will be.

Miss Gage is very gloomy and believes the Rockefeller people and the Yale people will refuse to continue the support if the place changes hands like that, which means I suppose the Yali governing board will recommend they discontinue the support for the present. That is where these people would be cutting off their noses to spite their faces for though they are supposed to be contributing something to support the hospital and therefore feel it is theirs; still the majority of funds come from outside and without them the place couldn't run. It is slightly what one might call disquieting and yet it is mighty interesting.

There is no doubt there is a very strong feeling and speculation about our getting out of here either entirely or for the time being within the next few weeks or months. Other Missions talk that way also. In fact there seems little sense staying on with Yale running as it is at present. For instance, 3 weeks ago they had a two-day holiday for Sun Yat-sen's birthday and then the next week they had 2 more for the Wanhsien affair, and then this week Monday was a holiday for something or other, and today and tomorrow. Now l ask you, what sort of decent work can any school do under circumstances like that? It would be a great deal better to close and save the expense until things get quieter and more normal and there is some assurance the schedule will not be interrupted.

The teachers who are trying to run laboratory courses are most upset and many of them find their students' work is not good between times. Mr. Leavens, the treasurer, has said many times he thinks our time of usefulness has about reached its end and it would be well to all pull out by June of next year. He has a good head and does not steam up over nothing.

His idea is Yali has been here for 25 years, has done good work, has many fine graduates throughout the country, has done well, and that it is finished for us. He may have the answer to it, and maybe not. Anyhow there is a spirit of unrest among all the people. Our nurses have it badly; particularly the men's nursing school. There is a slight foundation for the rumor, as the board recommended last year the men be replaced by women. I have had to be the goat in this case as Superintendent of Nurses.

It all came to a head at once when a number of men walked out so the women are now on the men's surgical ward. They are not very keen about it, and the men don't like the idea of having to go there just for unpleasant treatments and for night duty, but that is the way it stands presently.

A few days ago we decided to let two women probationers go who have been here for eight months and are not much good. We decided it at a faculty meeting attended by five Chinese instructors, as well as by us four foreigners. When the girls were told to go, all the others got excited and sent a delegation to Miss Gage asking just why it was and requesting they do not be sent away. They had heard through the woman instructor who was trying to smooth things out that we had insinuated things against their characters and that all was not said when we simply stated their work was not good enough. These are the days when the slightest sorts of thing arouse people, so the kids had a meeting last night.

Miss Beeby lives in a little "nubbin" as she calls it, on one side of the nurses' home and she said she was in bed and asleep when she heard all the row downstairs, and thinking that someone had come in to disturb the nurses, got up to go down to see what it was all about. She had heard several little ladies making speeches and then, to her surprise, some men's voices. All the men and women nurses, minus the graduates, were having a neat little meeting all of their own, with no older nurses and no faculty or anything like that present.

This is modern times and China is not the place it once was. We have ceased any sort of worry about the discretion of having women on the men's side now. The annoying part of that is that in normal times we could bawl them out for holding meetings like that after hours and with no faculty member present and all that sort of thing, but it is the thing now to disregard any sort of regulations, so we calmly (?) stand by and let them go to it.

Everyone admits it cannot go on for much longer like this. We agree that if the little ladies are inspired by outsiders to make any sort of unreasonable demands, we shall not consider them at all but tell them all to behave and do their stuff and then see what happens.

I heard the Middle School has sent in another lot of demands, 13 in number, including a reduction in tuition, a reduction of some teachers' salaries, and a demand for a new gymnasium before the next term! There are many teachers who have been longing for a new gym for years, and if the dear students can make one spring up by demanding it, then we are all for it. Of course, their instructions regarding what they demand have been received from the students' union outside.

One wonders what would have happened if none of the original demands had been acceded to in the first place. There were several on the faculty who were against granting any of them, and I heard they are all agreed not to give in on any of the present demands. Mr. Kwei, the brother-in-law of Mrs. Chang, says there is not one of them that any of us would consider. If they are after closing the school, they are following the proper tactics but I wonder if they are deluded into thinking the money would continue to come in from America. It's great dope and amazing to see how it works out.

The pathetic part of it all is that many students and other people, who are not in sympathy with all this business, are only interested in learning and studying and behaving themselves and yet are afraid to stand out against all the other students' unions. If they opposed, they would be written up in the newspaper and have all sorts of things said against them. They would rather die or go against their own principles than to have anything like that happen to them. It is the eternal problem of Chinese "face[70]." With all this going on, I wonder how any old buzzards like Pa Gowan will attempt to teach Chinese history. All I am writing will certainly be out of date by the time it reaches you. No one can possibly keep up with it and if one can believe what the papers say, things are not standing still in other parts of China either.

Now, just supposing we should close here, Jess and Nell and I have a swell plan: We shall take our return fares, pool our interests, and head for home going west. In Manila or Italy or France, or anywhere, we shall

---

70. "Face" is a Chinese social concept not hard to understand because, even as Westerners, everyone has face. When equated to Western values, face is very similar to the notion of reputation.

take turns getting nursing jobs so all the family money will not be running out, but there will be a slight income. It is quite possible this time of year the place would not be overrun with tourists, or adventuresses who would want to do the same thing. My only request is we got on so that I can be in New York by June to see my little brother do his stuff, and to get a ride home in case the family is still going to do that stunt. One might be inclined to find compensation in being driven out of a country. Fortunately, my contract with the Mission allows for return fare if I have to leave any time after June 1926. I guess it was wary old brother Leavens who put that in.

Will you be good enough to show this to Harold? I think he would be interested, to say the least. He may be the ultimate gainer by having gone home 5 years before his coworkers out here, as it will leave them in the same position he had were the school to close soon.

I do not feel particularly sorry for any of us except the Chinese staff members, those like Paul Kwei and others. He is a real Chinese gentleman and a believer in right and law and order and decency. Were this place to close, he would not have his country to return to, as we have, as he is already in it. He ranks with others who have had foreign advantages and education as "foreign slaves." It is not very pleasant for them to go down the streets and have that yelled at them, or to have themselves written up in the paper in these terms.

Speaking of newspapers, there is some ridiculous stuff printed therein. They tell me of an article a few days ago that says at the Hunan Yale Hospital, they charge $5 for a boy and only $1 for girl babies, and

"Down with Foreign Slaves," Chinese Involved with "Foreign Devils."

money is used to buy red eggs for the doctors. Red eggs are what they pass around instead of cigars. I asked our new obstetrician, a very cordial Chinese from Johns Hopkins, if that was an imperialistic doctrine he had inaugurated here; we never used to have that sort of thing before he came, "Ta Ta Ti Kuo Chu Ni," as they say, "Down with Imperialism."

They have posted those signs all over the city. That is one of the favorite sports now, along with parades and meetings. We have them at the hospital gate, and on the corners of the building. Also ones demanding an eight-hour day, and inviting the world to the Monday morning service, at 8 o'clock, in honor of Sun Yat-sen, also "Down with Imperialism." The Chinese seem to take this more in the spirit of "wan wan"—a good time—than as though they had a grudge. In fact, they are not a downtrodden race. They have not been browbeaten by generations of aristocrats, as were the French. One or two generations make or destroy a family's importance and there has been no great aristocracy opposing the poor proletariat. It's great dope.

December 3, 1926

From the Hospital Board to the School of Nursing. (in original syntax)

To the Delegates of the School of Nursing:

The Hospital Board has met, and considered your request of this morning about the retention of the four probationers. The Board is gratified that you are so loyal to your possible schoolmates and take such an interest in the welfare of your school.

It would say again to you what the Dean said this morning, and the faculty said in the letter of yesterday, that not keeping a student at the end of, or during probation simply is giving the student a chance to make good in another occupation but does not say anything against the character of the student. They would explain to you that:

Lei Chi Ch'en was only told that for his own good, to regain his health he should go away from the hospital atmosphere of sick people and rest until such time as classes with new students begin, next term and that then he was to return.

Lung Hsu Ch'eh was told that his average for two months in all of his studies was below 50%, his studies including ward work. Therefore he was advised not to waste his time here, but to take up at once other work, which he would enjoy more.

As for Miss Ch'ien and Miss Koh, their probation was extended at their earnest request. If they still want another chance to see whether or not they can make a success of nursing, we can give them another trial, and hope that their work will prove so interesting that their patients and fellow workers will all feel that they cannot be spared from the wards.

We trust that you will realize in this letter the Board's attempt to work with you for the best good of both patients and students - a double responsibility borne by all schools of nursing.

For the Hospital Board:

F. C. Yen, J. R. B. Branch, W.J. Hail, D.H. Leavens, F. S. Sung, N. D. Gage

December 5, 1926

This letter further demonstrates the challenges and attitudes Harriett, and other managers, encountered in operating the hospital and medical school. (In original syntax)

Letters to Patients

Changsha Nurses' Cooperative Association

5 Dec. 1926

Dear Friends:

We, the nurses of Hsiang-Ya have suffered deeply from the exactions of the Imperialists. Our woes have been intense, and we must tell them to you. Every day we study for four hours, and are on duty for eight and we receive no wages. But this is a mere detail. The most important power, which we should have, we have not. What power? That of meeting, speech, publication, strikes - all of these we have not. Ordinarily if two or three of us try to speak together we are not allowed to, but are separated. This is like the old days of public execution of those who spoke against the government. Should this be continued under the Republic? Under the Revolutionary Government the Hsiag Ya Hospital still uses this method!!

We have suffered persecution enough! Under the Revolution we will use our strength to get free. When shall it be? We know that we must unite and down the Imperialists. Not only the Imperialists, but their running dogs, the militarists, compradors[71], Government officials trying to take bribes, those who take money from the Imperialists and steal their country's property. Then we shall hare great good and pleasure from the Revolution. So the Labor Union tells us to resist these Imperialists. We hope the Revolution will help us. We have many watchwords:

Down with the Imperialists

Down with the running dogs

Protect the Kuomintang

Protect the Kuomintang Government

Protect the Central Labor Union

Get back the Hsiang-Ya Hospital

Down with those who oppress the nurses

Better nurses' conditions

Hurrah for the Changsha Nurses' Union

Hurrah for the Central Labor Union

Hurrah for the Hunan Provincial Labor Union.

We, the nurses, have been oppressed by the Imperialists, even beyond words. We have no other means but to rise against them. In this we have several important points:

I. We must oppose the Imperialists

2. We must be independent. They wish to push us further into the mire.

3. They wish you to leave the hospital so that they can close it.

After that we would have no further means of support. The Hunan Government gives much money to this institution. It is not the property of the Imperialists. Chinese must have something to say about this.

---

71. 1. An intermediary; a go-between. 2. A native-born agent in China and certain other Asian countries.

Because of this you should have something to say, and help us, and not listen to those who try to force you out of the hospital. We ask you to help us by not going.

We have great hopes of accomplishing our end, and ask you to excuse us for what discomfort yal may suffer.

Hsi and Ya Nursing Students

December 7, 1926 ~ Changsha

Dear Mother,

This is being written at 7:50 in the morning just after first morning rounds. To see the calm and mild way in which the nurses are all plodding around and the vigor with which the servants are sweeping the floors, one would never suspect there is the slightest reason for thinking that trouble ever came near our doors. But it was certainly sniffing at the keyhole. Yesterday, the nurses themselves brought trouble here, the poor deluded little creatures. I'll tell you how it has all been since the last time I wrote. I can't remember just when that last time was; it seems a long time ago, judged by events which have transpired since, but it is not so long.

There has been a bit of hell let loose, as it were, and I do not mean fire and brimstone and shoveling of coal but the more subtle kind wherein one sees one's efforts of years gradually coming to nothing and a structure which has taken a lifetime of hard work to build up toppling on its foundations. That is, the organization and morale of an institution like this. I think when I wrote last, the nurses were going in hard for meetings. That is always the preliminary to trouble, especially when nurses are kept up each night until 2 o'clock or so and then expected to do a decent day's work, and night nurses spend their days dashing about on important business.

Their first note was to demand the reinstatement of two women probationers who had been dropped after 8 months' trial because of poor ward work and poor classwork, and for two men probationers, one of whom was sent home to rest indefinitely, after a bad case of dysentery, and the other who was dropped for poor work and disobeying the dormitory rules.

The faculty had already decided to drop the kids, but the school committee—composed largely of some Yale people who have been harassed to death by the action of their students in the Middle School—decided to give in on the matter of women students and allow them another trial. We on the faculty were a bit peeved but decided we should say nothing more as we were quite sure this would only give them confidence of their great power and intimidation of us, enough to produce something more unreasonable.

Such was the case, for on Saturday morning, they sent in a series of demands. The preamble states how they are revolutionaries and eager to partake in the great movement that will overthrow all imperialism, and that they "have been prevented in the past by the anti-revolutionists who have had the authority to which they cling in fear. As an evidence of their fear, they used the poorest possible means in discharging our fellow-students, and we are so shameful we therefore make the following demands." Then follow the demands, thirteen in number. They ask for the reinstatement of four pupils, for free speech and all that, and for the right to attend patriotic meetings and parades. They demand the resignation of Dr. Chao, Staff Resident in Medicine, because he is imperialistic; they ask for added amahs (servants) on the women's wards, and for increases in their allowances. They want their books and uniforms to be furnished by the hospital outside of their allowances, and they do not have to pay for things they have broken. They expect to graduate in three years with no time counted out for unexpected leaves of absence to attend funerals and weddings, or as a result of sickness.

When Miss Gage saw them, she said she knew so well how they would be worded and what the answers were to be that she hardly needed to read them. They were the same sorts of things the Middle School asked for and were coached in practically the same terms. Oh yes, one more issue, there was to be a student representative on the faculty and no student is to be discharged without the Students' Union consent.

The committee who answered them said we were all anxious for them to be patriotic, and had neither forbidden them to attend any sorts of patriotic demonstrations, providing it did not interfere with care of patients or studies; that we all want them to be good nurses, and in doing so, they must consider first the patients' welfare, many of whom are revolutionary soldiers. The government in their educational regulations has never approved student representation. The matter of amahs and salaries and uniforms, being financial ones, are referred to the hospital, as well as the question of Dr. Chao. They might take less time to graduate, thereby not fulfilling the Nurses Association of China regulations, if they wish to lose their registration. They are not charged for breakage, and the matter of probationers has already been decided.

About the time the demands came in, I was becoming annoyed at the nerve of some students, who would either never appear on duty or walk off before their time, or disregard the time slips entirely. I therefore sent around a little notice with the time slips saying I expected them to remember their patients, and follow the time slips. I felt at last alone, dealing with the situation in the sternway it deserved.

About half an hour later, I happened to glance out my window and there were about half the entire nursing school going out to the classroom in the new nurses' home to have a meeting! Seldom have I felt so silly, or I might add, so disgusted. The kids spent most of the day having meetings of one sort or another, leaving only enough nurses on duty to hand out a few medicines and take a few temperatures. I felt so definitely on Saturday the place is finished—it is only a matter of a few weeks until we must close—that I went gaily off to a party to forget a bit about it. I found out the Branches had done the same. It really was quite a relief, and I now feel a great sympathy for old man Nero. I think justice has never been done. If Rome was burning, what better could he do than sit on the top of his house and fiddle? I came home quite late and as has been my custom, went around the hospital to see what was doing, or who was doing it. The first thing that greeted my eyes was a multitude of posters, about 6 inches wide and 18 inches long in all sorts of colors—red ones, yellow ones, blue ones, purple ones, orange ones, and whatnot. They were plastered all over the walls, beside and on our office doors; it was impossible to look in any direction and not see them. Their inscriptions were mostly, "Down with Imperialism," "Down with Capitalism," "Out with Dr. Chao" "Take back our fellow students," and the like.

It seems this is a very serious form of insult; that it is hard to understand the real significance of them to the Chinese mind. To us, it all seems so much like child's play, but, after all, they are like children. I found two nurses were not on duty at all, and the doors were all open between wards. There can be no such thing as locked doors in this great and free country. I was surprised to see the chief agitator's flying coat-tails, as the men nurses disappeared around the corner into the women's private ward. He soon came out looking rather wild, and as he passed me, I remarked he was up rather late. He replied, "I am very tired." I told him I should think he would be and that he had better go to bed. That remark probably stamped me as an Imperialist. Everything we do and say these days proves to them we are Imperialists and Capitalists.

Sunday they seemed to be on duty all right but gained speed as the day progressed, handing in a second lot of demands about noon. That is going true to form, as that is the program followed by the middle school students who demanded in their second demands they be given a new gymnasium before next semester. In the second nurses' demands, they first asked for Miss Gage's removal, then that the proctor be dismissed, then all the nurses who are now seniors be graduated in two months and be kept on for a year at a salary of $60 a month. They now get $20 for the first year. They ask for more servants in the hospital, for higher allowance for nurses, and no time be taken off their course as a result of the present storm, and no student be "revenged on" for the present agitation. The others I can't remember. They are not worth remembering.

The feeling among the foreigners on the board was to tell them none of their demands could even be considered for a minute, but the Chinese felt we should go more easily so answered them more carefully, but did not grant any of them. We wondered what would happen next, expecting them to walk out at any time. The Medical School had had a big meeting and the Medical students declared their loyalty to the institution and their intention of staying on. They are in a sad position because it is so evident by the mere fact they are here, they want a good medical education, and yet they are unable to influence the labor people, or whoever the agitators are, to keep the nurses quiet.

Monday morning they were all present and accounted for but threatened to go out on strike at noon. We were prepared and discharged most patients. Then nurses and coolies were supposed to all go out together. However, I heard the Union had told them their duty lay toward the poor sick and suffering and so they themselves decided who should be on and who should be off, so there was one nurse on most wards most of the time. In between times, we ourselves helped.

In the morning, a delegation of insolent little nurses came to Miss Gage's office and demanded the YMCA money, saying they had the president's signature, but they couldn't get it from the treasurer without Miss Gage's check. She allowed them $10 and they were so mad they called us all robbers and acted shamefully toward her. I was in the office at the time and it was all I could do to keep from kicking them out bodily. Meetings of all sorts are held at all sorts of times. The nurses had a big parade yesterday afternoon, banners flying, and all the other nurses dragged in and yelling "Down with Imperialism" and "Out with the foreign slaves," and all that.

When they returned, they announced themselves with the orphan band blaring its worst and a salute of firecrackers such as I have never heard at any funerals or weddings since I've been here. It was for all that, that they wanted the $75 Y. money. The poor deluded creatures.

Through it all, it is intensely interesting to see the play of foreign versus Chinese methods and temperaments. Among the executives, they are anxious to compromise and smooth things over, granting requests when they can, and putting off others. The Chinese members seem to carry it to an extreme. The last set of demands were so absolutely impossible the foreign members were all for bringing things to an issue by telling them "All right, go and strike," but the Chinese members persuaded them to compromise and stall.

Mr. Yen resigned as Hospital Superintendent and Dr. Branch was elected in his place. However, Dr. Yen hangs around and gets into things as before. One reason why the foreigners have been so lenient and have given way to the Chinese's judgment is they did not want to hurt Dr. Yen, or seem to be disloyal to him. We seem to have such a poor deluded sense of loyalty, we foreigners, that I am sure the Chinese do not understand it, as they just pack up and depart when they are in a tight pinch, rather than sticking by an individual to whom they should feel a sense of loyalty. We have all felt anxious to bring it to an issue so we could feel definitely how things stand, but with this tantalizing, nerve-wracking, and stalling business, it is impossible. It is difficult to know just what is the wise and proper course when we are trying to cooperate with the Chinese.

If we were in a business firm, we would have told them all to go to the devil long before this. We wonder if that wouldn't be the proper course now, because certainly as far as the nurses and patients are concerned, neither are profiting by the present way of things. The nurses are being given too much consideration to affairs not worth of considering, and they are doing all sorts of sloppy work on the wards, and we do not know how much we can discipline and reprimand them; because of the board's attitude we must not do anything to precipitate matters.

Most of us would like to precipitate something, rather than going on as at present, for certainly we cannot continue for long this way and the break is absolutely certain to come and we should like to be fresh to meet it. They tell us today if we allow the nurses to strike, the coolies and all other workers will strike not only here, but also throughout the city. We should hate to cause inconvenience to others in that way and I think they would not blame us, but thank us for crystallizing the thing causing trouble among the missions and business houses. As I say, it is dead sure to come somewhere, sometime, soon, and I think it might as well be here.

The latest idea is that Dr. Yen and Mr. Tsao will go and talk personally with Chiang Kai-shek, who is supposed to be in Hankou. That brings up the political situation here in the province. It seems to be the consensus that the leaders here at present do not represent the constructive element of the Kuomintang, but are the Communist wing, which was kicked out of Canton and sought their way here. They are the most radical outfit of all. There seems to be a difference of opinion of why they are tolerated here.

One is that Chiang Kai-shek and the other leaders are so busy in the North with their military campaign that they have no time or men to spare to come here and keep order. Therefore, they are keeping their hands off for the time being, particularly as Hunan is the logical connecting province between Kwangtung and Hupeh[72]; and, they

---

72. A province in Central China.

don't want to risk losing their hold by antagonizing the Communists. Perhaps they can resist them when they come back, start a new order, or cut off their line of communication.

The opinion seems to be that when they have finished their military exploits in the North and east they will have time to retrace their steps and arrange matters here. It is with that view that they, Dr. Yen and Mr. Tsao, will approach the men in Hankou and see what they can do about it. My opinion is he will not have the time or the power to immediately end our difficulties as this labor union stuff is too well organized and too powerful at present to have the word, telegraphed or written of even General Kiang himself, carry much weight. I may be mistaken.

As for the nurses themselves, they are in a sad way, the poor children. About 80% of them are interested in nothing except learning to be good nurses, and having their examinations and diplomas. Many of them don't know what the demands were or that there was a second lot of them handed in. They are told to walk off, so they walk off, and then are told to come back, so they come back. It is the mysterious "they" who tells them to do these things. I have tried to find out who "they" are, but the nurses say it is "other people," which is equally indefinite.

The saddest element is the fact they are terrorized into doing or not doing by the threat of "da." The word means to hit, and is what mobs yell when they want to beat up someone. The ludicrous part of the power of the word is the Chinese are not given to hitting one another; they seldom fight, in our sense of the word, so they probably don't know what it means. Maybe it's fear of the unknown?

At the same time that may explain why they attach such significance to it. I pinned one nurse down to ask just what it was she was afraid of in being "da"-ed, and she said they would put a cap of shame on her head, tie a rope around her neck, and lead her through the streets with a sign on her that she was a foreign slave, and then all the people would yell at her. Isn't that pathetic? It is the power of that threat that will take them off duty, make them parade through the streets for an afternoon, and make them fear to stand up for what they believe to be right. They would rather lose their immortal soul than to lose face.

I really think this face business is the answer to the largest part of the situation. The posters were put to make us lose face and they are going to lose a lot themselves when they have to take them down, as they will most certainly have to do if I am to stay on here. They don't want to do all these crazy things they have been doing the last few days and yet they are afraid not to. When so many of them went off parading yesterday afternoon, even our graduates went, for fear someone would come and "da" them if they did not go.

I am quite convinced of the outcome and yet as you know I am not what you would call a pessimistic person, and that is that we must close. If they attach so much importance to this face business, I wonder what they think of Miss Gage's insults this past week, and to others of us to a lesser degree. If they are willing to work in the hospital and resume classes in the nursing school, they will have to begin again on the same terms which they accepted when they came in, except for revisions which have been granted in the demands. That means we shall be able to discharge probationers and other nurses when we think they should go and they are to do their ward duties according to their assignments. The whole thing came to a head over our discharging two probationers who will be renewed in about a month when we have our final exams and let the ones go who have failed in their classes and ward work; that is, if they are consistent and stick by their student union business which does not want a student dismissed without the union consent.

They do not seem to get the idea probationers are not nurses from the very meaning of the word. The point is, the nurses are in the unique position of being on duty in the hospital as well as being students in the nursing school. As hospital employees, they are in the same social classes as the amahs and coolies is a bit of a joke, because they are better than the servants and consider themselves better also. The poor kids are unfortunate victims of the revolution.

We feel confident about our kind friends, who have been contributing support to the place and have been maintaining the nursing school with this business. They will be leery of sinking any more money into such a place, as much for their treatment of Miss Gage as for any other reason. Most give because of admiration and friendship for her and because of her influence and I'm sure I have not the heart at present to urge any one to send gifts to a place which seems to be doing its best to get rid of us, break up the institution which we have built, and renounce our way of education.

Miss Gage herself hopes she will be sent home, and will leave before long I am sure, in any case. She says she has lost all her self-respect, and I am sure we have lopped off bits of ours besides losing a great deal of temper and developing blood pressures from restraining our anger! I have tried to make totally clear the thing is engineered by only a few students in the school itself and by outside influences. How much is Russian we have no way of knowing and what is their purpose is another hard question to answer. We don't know whether their idea is to get rid of foreigners entirely or to turn the place over to their cohorts to run as a medical school, hospital and nursing school according to their ideas. I imagine the ultimate aim is something like that.

Phil Greene says the idea is that here is a big, fine, well-organized institution going well, and they have absolutely had no hand in it. That will never do. Everything must be under the Kuomintang. Therefore it must be got rid of entirely, or come under their influence so they can point at it and say, "Here is an example of what we are doing for education in China." This may be the situation.

It is hard to tell at such close range. They seem to overlook that so much money comes from America and this particular group of donors would not care to subscribe to a place run by any other type of people than those in here at present. I think they believe the treasurer's report to be false as theirs would be, were they publishing a statement of finances. They put a sign on the treasurer's door, "The official who takes bribes." It is a regular slogan and he thought it quite a joke. They're just now going on parade so bring on the orphan band and let's celebrate.

Merry Christmas and Happy New Year.

December 11, 1926 ~ Changsha

Dear Mother,

Comparatively speaking, things have been happening slowly here the past few days. The nurses have not gone on strike; at least they do not call it such. They are all on duty in the mornings but in the after-noons, if there happens to be a meeting or a parade, they all dash off or are directed by the Students' Union as to which ones should stay on duty. It is slightly awkward as half the time they do not leave enough people, or they make night duty people get up for afternoon work and all that sort of thing.

A few days ago we were told there is to be a sort of truce for two weeks. There are those who say for three weeks, but I think they are a bit off. The two weeks is supposed to be the time allowed for Tang Yen Kai to get here from Canton. He is the boy who was here as Governor before Chao Hang Ti, and whom Chao deposed. He has joined up with the Kuomintang and is one of their big guns. He is the one who wrote the characters to be enlarged and put up over our hospital entrances, indicating this is the Hsiang-Ya Hospital and we have two pictures of him in the front hall. I think the truce was managed by Dr. Yen, his idea being that after Tang gets here we can close the hospital and then open it again under reformed management if that seems the thing to do. At least Dr. Yen is one of the original parties and an influential man who can assist in whatever is to be done. Perhaps the Kuo Min Tan counts on him to sponsor their cause, and perhaps he will. In any case, we are all marking time until the day arrives and then there will be some more fireworks, I suppose.

Dr. Yen is on the verge or over the edge of a nervous breakdown. They said a few days ago, before he resigned, he had not slept for six nights and was in such a sad way they did not know what to do with him. He could not remember what he had said two minutes before and kept repeating himself and was altogether quite pitiful.

Since then he has had some rest and seems to be better, but is still stirring things up in the vain hope of saving the pieces of the hospital. I do not know whether Mr. Tsao has gone or not. He has been lurking around in the city somewhere, though officially he is out of the hospital for the time being. I rather think he counts on Tang Yen Kai doing something in the reinstatement line, though I hardly see how that can be done unless he is willing to join the Tang. Maybe he will do so if Yang thinks he should. Perhaps Tang represents a more conservative wing and it would not be so inconsistent as if he were to join the ranks of Tang as it now stands. I have understood they cannot belong to the Party and to the YMCA at the same time and anyone as sincerely a

Christian as Yen or Tsao could hardly give up their religion. However, strange things have been arranged in the past few months, so we are not surprised at anything anymore.

The Middle School went on a strike last week and they began to hear rumors of unrest in the college. The faculty met and thought to get the jump on them a bit by declaring a winter vacation. They had the notice all ready to post and then Mr. Hail thought it wise to go to the Foreign Office and find out what they would do in a case like having the students refuse to go.

While he was gone at the office, the students had a meeting and decided to go on strike. So strike they did, and the college is also closed. It is too bad there was a delay, for now they cannot get the kids to go home. They hang around all the time, playing basketball or having meetings and eating rice. No one knows just what the outcome will be, though I understand Mr. Hail has had a communication from the central Student Union declaring there will be a general strike if the students' demands are not granted at once. I do not know what the demands are, but suppose they are like the others who have come from various schools everywhere; student representation on the faculty, forbidding the faculty to discharge a student without the consent of the union, and all that. I hope for once they do not grant the kids what they want, but take a firm stand. I am certain all the other schools in the city would be grateful for someone starting a precedent of dealing with the situation with a firm hand. It will have to be dealt with eventually, and it might as well be sooner in the minds of most people. They say all the other schools are waiting to see what Yali does. As the largest school, it has the lead.

Our nurses unfortunately are in a very poor state of morale. Russian fashion, I suppose it is, for them to have completely disregarded all the regulations of the new Nurses' Home. They have taken over the "parlor," as it were, for a head office of their local division head and this youth sits there all day with any number of the other nurses about, both men and women. Very chummy and informal!

You may remember one demand was that they be given more freedom of speech; Miss Gage had previously not allowed any communication between the men and women students. They are now making up for it by being too chummy for any words. You doubtless wonder why in blazes we stand for it. I wonder myself sometimes, but it is mainly because of our rather queer position here. Being partly controlled by the Chinese, in theory at any rate, we have to adopt their way of handling things which is largely that of watchful waiting and compromise and writing letters.

I think President Wilson must have had Chinese inclinations in him somewhere. So many of his policies are recalled at this time in the handling of the situation. However, I am glad the Chinese are so constituted, rather than like their leaders, the Russians. It is a great deal pleasanter to have them holding meetings and talking all night if they want to, rather than out on the streets mowing down the populace with machine guns.

It is quite evident to all of us that the Nursing School cannot go on at the present rate. We are all unanimous in that. That is, if they want us to stay and help here and they cannot get along without us at the present rate, the way the hospital funds are arranged, and considering the support from America. I think if later they want to run it according to their own ideas, I for one should not stay here. They might be able to recruit some other foreign nurses if they want them, but for us who have been here under the present regime, it would be practically impossible. I think, however, there is no denying the fact it would be interesting to see how it all works out and I might be tempted to stay and see, if I did not care for my own face. It is the sort of opportunity that would have its attractive side, adventurously at least.

3 p.m. I have just heard from Dr. Branch that the nurses say they cannot accept his conditions under which they were to work in the hospital from now on. That included a return, more or less, to the former way of running things with Miss Gage as Dean of the school and the reinstatement of proctors. It also included apologies, which they say they cannot make. They are quite right; that is, if they are consistent, they cannot apologize for what they have done as union members and they cannot go back on their new organization either.

The great and sad nurses' error was when they joined the labor union. I don't know why they did that except they must have been driven to it somehow from the outside. Of course, they are workers in the hospital, and students in the nursing school, so I suppose they have a perfect right to join two unions. It means a double expense and makes the coolies mad because they have had a certain honor in their ranks and they feel the nurses do not really belong there.

Which reminds me of the poster business. Branch declared all the posters that had been put up all over the hospital should be taken down. They were put up by the nurses and taken down by the coolies. All brothers together, but rather peevish brothers if one could guess from the look on the coolies' faces, as they scrubbed the walls. The next day, the coolies put up some very large posters, quite inoffensively, asking Dr. Yen to return to the hospital as Superintendent. Then, for fear we might not understand, they put up some in English declaring:

We sincerely expect Dr. Yen's restoration at once.
Hsiang-Ya Coolie Union

The spelling is an exact copy. I thought it rather cute of them to write it in English and it shows how they have profited by the coolie school we have had at night.

Other institutions are getting it in the neck also. The Hunah Bible Institute figures largely in the papers now. We wondered if the students there would protest against the Bible study, but the tactics have been of a different nature. They say dreadful things about the morals of the place which has both men and women students. They hoped to have Antoinette Black to head the women's part of the Hospital, I may have told you. They say the matron is not really a matron but there to get these girls who are for the men students' pleasure. It is really quite sickening and the one way that would hurt Dr. Keller most. The worst they say about Dr. Hsiao is he drinks coffee—with milk in it! We wonder if he eats bread with butter on it.

In a pamphlet distributed to the populace, our nurses declare we are all imperialists and do not know their language. We stand up before them in class and open and shut our mouths but they understand nothing of what we say. This pamphlet and poster business is great stuff. It would be of more importance were they not doing it in every other school in the city as well.

Do be a bit discreet in the matter of broadcasting my contributions. I'd hate to be run out as a foreign spy. I write in detail for your declaration and for the interest of Harold and Dwight who've been here and know the people. Will you be good enough to keep the letters for reference as it is the nearest I come to a diary. If we continue to feel as unhappy over the situation as we're inclined to do now, we won't feel much enthusiasm over the speechmaking business when we get home.

December 13, 1926 ~ Changsha

(Not sent, but indicative of Miss Gage's thinking.)

TO THE STUDENTS OF THE HSIANG-YA SCHOOL OF NURSING
AND PROBATIONERS:

In order to give you a chance to continue your nursing education, the faculty has decided that if you meet the following conditions within twelve hours the school will continue. Otherwise you will be considered to have withdrawn yourselves from the school, and will be expected to return to your homes at once:

1. There must be an apology to Dr. Yen, Miss Huang and Mr. Wen and all your teachers for your discourtesy and unmannerly conduct in many ways during the past few days.

2. A request to the teachers to begin teaching, with the names of the students who desire this signed.

3. The men are not to go to the women's dormitory, or to the wards staffed by women nurses, nor the women to the men's quarters without permission from the supervising nurse on duty,

4. The proctors are to be retained.

5. Every pupil is to be understood, as heretofore to be on probation until graduation.

6. A change of name of the new Student Union from Hu Sui Lien Ho Hui to Kan Hu Lien Ho Hui.

7. A spirit of willing obedience is to be shown in accepting duty assignments or correction of the wards, as it should

be realized that these are given only to help the student become a better nurse. A great improvement in the work of everyone must be shown.

8. A pupil dismissed for infringement of rules of inability to carry the work is not to think that he is being discriminated against.

9. A return to the former rules of the school as to behavior and duty.

10. Repair the damage done to the School of Nursing - bolts loosened, chains broken, etc.

Nina D. Gage, for the faculty,

December 17, 1926 ~ Changsha

Dear Mother,

There has been a post office carriers' strike here for the past few days so I have not bothered to send a letter along knowing it would not get out. We have for so long had uncertain mail, we forget there is such a thing. The result is we have a happy surprise every time some comes in. Fat chance! There's nothing to be done about it apparently but to pursue the watchful waiting policy we have all had to adopt and which is steadily getting all our goats.

Here in the hospital things are, on the surface, not much changed but underneath things do boil. Every now and then they burst to the top and we get an idea of turmoil. They decided at the end of last week the hospital must close; things couldn't go on as they have been going. Therefore, official permission was given by the Yali governing board to the hospital board to close the place. That sounded good to all of us.

Then the nurses sent a list of their conditions under which they wished the nursing school to run. Much the same things they had demanded before. We have been fed up to the teeth with the way things have gone and even Dr. Branch, who is now the hospital superintendent, agreed it was not good to have the nursing school so utterly demoralized and the kids running around at all hours of day and night, the men in the women's dormitory and the women in the men's for meetings at any old time. So in the hospital board meeting they decided to close the nursing school and posted a notice to the effect that in view of the conditions presented by the nurses, the board found it impossible to decide at once what the school's future was to be; therefore we would consider the school as closed temporarily and the students were to go home.

The idea was to get them scattered and then to open up again in a few weeks or months under what would be agreeable conditions to everyone. With that in view, we moved the patients from 5 wards into 3 and staffed them, somewhat inadequately with graduate nurses, thinking we, ourselves, with the aid of extra coolies and orderlies from the other closed wards, would be able to care for the patients, certainly as well as they have been cared for lately.

However, did the nurses obediently pack up their baggage and get out? Like fun they did. They all not only stayed but most of them were on the wards in uniform. I cannot say they were on duty—that would be an insult to nursing service. However, there they were, and there was apparently no getting rid of them.

We had told a few girls and one man to get out before this notice was posted. Three women did get away in time and before the others were wise to what they were doing, but two girls were too slow and the poor little man didn't get away either. His attempted departure was amusing to look back upon, but not quite so humorous as annoying at the time. I saw him scuttling down the stairs with a big bed roll on one arm and a huge basket full of books, foreign shoes, and washing paraphernalia, as well as many other possessions on the other arm. He was making rapid tracks for the door and a couple of rickshaws when I saw one ex-pupil at the entrance having an altercation with him. This lad had been in a few days before with a long face and had told Jess how he had to get out by the beginning of the month because he knew this trouble was coming and he would have to be in it if he stayed and he didn't want to be in it. Evidently that was just a bit of good acting so that if she saw him there at the door, near where her office is located, she would suspect nothing, for evidently he is a picket and tried to prevent the nurse from getting away.

I saw them having a row outside, so I dashed out in the rain and tried to prevent him from grabbing the kid's baggage. It was hardly a ladylike procedure, but I was so peeved I did not stop to think about the seemliness of it. Just as I was making some headway against the little brat, another of our tough troublemakers appeared and the two of them threatened the rickshaw coolies so they put down their rickshaws and the game was up. I took the boy's baggage and his basket and I ditched them in Jess's office, thinking I would send them to him somewhere in the city later in the day. He seemed to be entirely discouraged himself and felt it was no use, and he had probably brought more trouble to himself. I am very much afraid that that is the way it will prove to be. He has now definitely stamped himself as being apart from them, instead of cooperating in their way of doing things. The answer is he is a dumbbell undoubtedly and has already taken 4 years to do 3 years of work. He just can't pass exams without trying them 4 or 5 times, but he has the most amazing amount of persistence.

The final exams for the Nurses Association of China came on the 3rd of January, and he is crazy to take them again, naturally, and says he will have "no face" at all before his father if he does not take them and pass this time. If we are still here we shall certainly see he takes them; otherwise send him to the hospital at Yueyang to take them. It means as much as State Board does to us at home.

In all this crazy business, it is very interesting to see how the Kuomintang policies and plans work out. I have had the organization somewhat explained to me and it clears up a lot of things that have been happening here. It seems each district or section is organized under a committee of five. This committee meets secretly every two weeks and decides what their attitude is to be on certain subjects connected with the institution or school or firm where they happen to be.

In this council of five they may express their opinions but after the decision is made, they must stick to it outside, work for it and devote their energies to carrying it through no matter what their private opinions may have been. If they go against the decision, they risk having their names taken from the lists and then they can no longer be party members; they themselves suffer and so do their parents. If they are Hunanese, they say they cannot dare be out of the party and expected to get along in the province.

It's a great game of terrorizing really. Everyone fears to stand out against it so they all try to get in it. Apparently they have to do some stunt to get in if they have in the past done anything which might be interpreted as against the party. If they can rouse a parade or present some good demands or something like that, then it seems they have won their laurels and can be readmitted to the ranks. It seems to be so definitely a permanent thing that it has them all in its grip.

It is a wonderful organization and apparently leaves no room for any opposition. Of course, they have the press under their supervision so nothing detrimental appears in the papers.. All their propaganda posters appear there and in large posters on the streets and in handbills passed out by "paraders." We have posters on our front wall and there are many on the Presbyterian Compound wall. One rather amusing one says, "Presbyterian Mission School, foreign slave girl factory. A-men," and then signed in English "J. Lingle," who is the school head.

They are fortunate there in having closed their school peacefully a few days ago before there was any noise of a strike. The girls were allowed to go, and they almost all cleared out in tears. The foreigners there will probably go home, as the conditions under which they will reopen under the new government are they are not to teach any religion whatsoever, whether voluntary or compulsory. After all, if you take that away from a Mission School, what is left? There is a great deal of speculation when they could open again but it is so indefinite and it looks now as though it would be a matter of months and perhaps years, so it would be better in the end for the foreigners to clear out and wait for the people to ask us to come back again.

Yali was officially closed, fortunately before they received a communication from the Educational Association telling them henceforth no mission schools will be allowed to close.

The students are still there as are our nurses. Their policy is to stick to the place and refuse to go, rather than getting mad and departing in a huff. You would know this is China. Everything's done backwards. Our big stunt now is to try to close the hospital, but we seem as far from it as we were a week ago. They have instructed the patients to refuse to go, and the interns are afraid to sign their discharges, so they linger on and the nurses prowl around the wards.

December 19, 1926 ~ Changsha

Dear Mother,

Here's another day, and of course, new developments. There was a threatened strike of nurses and hospital coolies, and even a suggestion all the foreigners' servants would also go out. It has reached the point now where some of us wish the bluff would be called, and they would go out. It's tiresome business being scared at the thought of being left without servants and then going ahead to compromise, lose a face, and have tiffin prepared as usual. There was a very lengthy and stormy meeting on Friday evening, called by the hospital board head, a Chinese named Tsao Tze Koo. He has been connected with hospital affairs for a long time and. according to what everyone says, is so crooked he couldn't spit straight. He made off with so much Educational Association funds and squeezed so much from building the new boulevard around the city wall that he couldn't leave town when this new Canton outfit came in.

He decided to get religion last summer but no Mission would take him in because he had just acquired a concubine and it seemed a bit irregular. I suppose she is now union head so his rating is going up. He has not been a Kuomintang member but I think sees his opportunity to get in with them if he can arrange it so they will get the hospital. He had all sorts of ideas at the meeting for compromise and giving in to the nurses, but Miss Gage had a list of irreducible minimum on which we had all agreed, so there was apparently nothing to do. Finally, Tsao said he would act as Dean of the Nursing School with Miss Gage as his private advisor! If you knew the man, you would know how absurd it is.

Miss Gage has become so tired with the affair and so discouraged and disgusted with the way things have gone that she agreed only too gladly, seeing there a way to shift the responsibility and have a chance to go home. That is her goal now, as it is for most of the rest of us also.

The prospect is he will agree and conciliate with the nurses, and do anything to keep peace in the family, but what will happen to the paltry nursing school funds that are so painfully and tryingly pried loose from kind friends at home is another matter. They all think we want to stay here because we are making such a good thing out of it for ourselves. For that is what the majority of them would be doing. They probably do not believe Miss Gage has guarded the funds with so carefully and stingy a hand all these years for the sake of making them go far, but just because she is mean and wants to make them suffer. That is the state of mind into which they have worked themselves.

She feels that when New Haven hears the affair's details and realizes how the funds are to be administered, by whom and what for, they will probably discontinue their support and send for us to come home. There is a sad joke there on us, because most of us haven't more than enough in the bank to get us to Shanghai. Those who were due to go home this summer on furlough are also at a loss, because they suspect they will receive no Yale Mission salary for the next year which would seem highly probable. So it goes. I wonder how all this dope will strike people at home. It is inconceivable to think of it happening anywhere in the world but in China. I presume after a few months or years it will all seem like a very funny nightmare to most of us, but at present, though unquestionably amusing, it is also a bit trying on the nerves.

We went on a shopping expedition yesterday and found the shops willing and eager to sell to us even though we were foreigners. I "pawn-shopped" to the extent of a couple of dressing case boxes sort of things, which are hard to describe, but which are very beautiful and ought to be acceptable gifts at home.

December 20, 1926 ~ Changsha

Dear Hank,

I've been pondering for a couple of days whether and what I ought to write to you for fear of being previously perhaps reckless, but in view of a sort of promise or agreement we made, I hereby spill the news. The answer is I am going to marry Charlie Keller. There now, ponder on that for a while. Did I write you once a few weeks ago in a jesting spirit about it?

To tell the truth, it was just a merry idea I happened to have. It has all of a sudden become much more than that and we're well away. The only flaw seems to be, he has never received actual word from his lawyer that his previous affair is finished, though everything should have been fixed last June.

That's the reason we're saying absolutely nothing about it to anyone. I've got to tell someone or bust. You doubtless think I'm what might be

called fickle or frivo-
lous or something,
considering last sum-
mer's madness. You
must give me credit
for having realized it
all the time. It was not
an affair I've been par-
ticularly proud of but
was what one might
call inevitable, and a
good experience—
better then than later.
I have a hunch Charlie
won't leave time for

Harriet and Charlie R. Keller, to Marry

any fool-business like that and I'll endeavor to do the same for him.
All right—don't be hasty—I'll tell you all about him. Glad to.

He's about my height; husky, inclined to be what I regret to say
might be called fat. That condition won't last after he's been under my
care for a while. His hair is black and his eyes blue, which is a pleasant combination. I'm not exactly sure how old he is —26, we think—a
mere detail. It means he's still kid enough to be full of prunes and crazy
as the deuce at times; matches my own moments of dippiness. At the
same time, his experiences of the past few years have matured him and
sobered him and balanced him wonderfully.

He knows what the marriage game means, needless to say, the
demands it makes on patience and forebearance. The result is I do not
feel I'm taking a leftover, but one who's wiser and finer for the experiences of youth. He's the one who is getting the small end of the deal,
when you consider how really on the verge of being an old maid I am.

Our plans are a bit foggy, due chiefly to the uncertain state of the
mission. The college, middle school and school of nursing are closed
due to Soviet, Kuomintang propaganda. It looks as though foreign
nurses would be recalled by the New Haven office and sent home, which
would be all right. The academic side is trying to run on until Chinese
New Year vacation in January and then close for the rest of the year.

Charlie is due for furlough in June but whether the mission will allow him next year's furlough salary with the prospect of his not returning is another matter. They'll probably have a hemorrhage when he appears with another wife. What I'd like to do would be to have us sent home say in February with return passage for both paid and salaries until June. I think the mission will do that. We could be married just before we leave and browse around to New York by way of Europe. We'd go to Cleveland where his family lives and then return to New Haven for Dwight's Commencement in June. My family should come out, too. By that time our funds will probably be so low we'll grab jobs, earn a bit of money, and then dig in for the winter. Charlie expects to get his M.A. He's a wonderful highbrow, Phi Beta Kappa, second man in his class, brains enough to make up for my lack. Everything looks rosy enough and crazy enough to suit us well. It all savors of what my family would call rather trashy but it's great stuff just the same. There's many a slip I know but we'll hope for no more slips anymore.

Now your part in this little affair might be to send me some decent jersey silk shirts and bloomers or panties to meet when I go down river to Shanghai. The post office is so rocky; it's no use sending packages up here and don't think I can hold together till I get downriver. A dress might do but don't send anything until I tell you definitely. If you buy a trousseau like Mademoiselle what's-her-name, I'll give you a peacock fan or something equally swell and elegant.

All I ask is, do, for the love of Mike and me, keep this under your hat. I'll let it out when the time comes. Don't tell a soul. Be good and you'll be lonesome. Joyfully.

December 21, 1926 ~ Changsha

Dear Jo,

I hope mother has kept you informed of progressing events in Changsha. I try to write home about it as much for future reference for myself as for actual telling of events. The whole business has been so sort of quaint, the sort of thing that would happen nowhere else in the world than China.

For instance, let me tell you of the Nursing School presently, and then you compare it to the institution where you are. We closed the school officially on the 15th, after a couple of weeks of discussion and repeated demands from the students about increases in allowance, less work, more servants, student control of the school, appeal to the union for everything, and all the rest of it. The morning we closed the school there were still pupils on duty though I had arranged for the wards to be covered by graduates with the assistance of coolies and amahs. The nurses stayed on the wards that day and have been on ever since. I cannot insult my profession by saying they have been on duty. You would hardly call it that, but at least they were there in person. That is the new idea when a school closes or goes on strike.

The pupils do not march out in a body. They stick in a body and nothing can pry them loose. They ran wild over the dormitory and behaved in unseemly manner, even in the eyes of hard-boiled western-ers. So there we were with the school closed, the nurses supposedly on their way home, and not one of them gone, and most of them on the wards. They had the poor taste to ally themselves with the labor union as well as the students' union so they had the coolies on their side and the power of a threatened general strike to intimidate us. Apparently it has been successful in terrorizing us because we have pursued a mild policy, as well as we could, in the vain effort to avoid trouble and act like Christians. Finally, the committees on the question of the nursing school reached a deadlock, *we* insisting on certain terms of discipline and authority and *they* insisting on their demands, which included disposing of Miss Gage and reducing the authority of the rest of us.

One of their main points (see directive on page 143) is that the faculty shall not have the power to discharge students without the consent of the rest of them and their union.

Did you ever hear of anything more impossible as trying to run a decent training school? You would think that some poor probationers were a sacrament that wasn't to be desecrated; no matter how many overdoses they give the patients, or babies to wrong mothers, etc. Finally the head Chinese on the hospital board said that he would take over, as official school head and he would give the orders and Miss Gage and the rest of us would act through him. I had a meeting with him yesterday in my official capacity as Superintendent of Nurses. I told him we had too many nurses and too many probationary students and some of them were not worth the poison it would take to kill them. Still, we are powerless to fire them unless they do something they consider terrible enough to warrant dismissal. He was so upset and so absolutely ignorant of the first details of a nursing situation that I was sorry for him. The outcome was I am to assign nurses to their duty, as many or as few as I like. Therefore I made out a list of nurses who are to be on duty for a week, leaving off all the poor ones and the probationary entirely. His idea is that at the end of a week we shall change to another group, while the other two-thirds rest and eat and raise bills for the school. Crazy isn't the name for it. It cannot possibly last, though in fact it hasn't begun yet. They didn't post my list of nurses for some reason I have yet to ferret out. We were terribly restless about it last week, but have adopted the Chinese attitude of watchfully waiting. The patients in the hospital are, fortunately not sick. They were all instructed by pamphlets, passed out by the nurses, they were to refuse to go home, that discharging them was just our way of taking bread out the poor nurses mouths. Then the interns were instructed not to discharge anyone. Therefore all these people linger around and have a pleasant rest in the wards. They have been instructed to admit no more patients through the office, but I notice they fill up when anyone dies or goes home in spite of them. It is all a vicious circle for the nurses are not receiving any instruction in the classroom and the patients are getting poor care on the wards. We have no hope of keeping school much longer. It will all probably come out in the wash. And, so will we, but I hope we get out with pure hands and a clean heart.

Charlie Keller has been on the verge of resigning several times but the middle school and college are still closed so he may be spared the responsibility. He was teaching economics and history and made some statements about the way things had worked out in other countries in that line and it happened they were not quite in accord with the teachings of Sun Yat-sen so they all got peeved and talked about making Charlie apologize. His brand of social science is not adapted to the Kuomintang. He has spent so much time in the past trying to know the students better, I think he knows them only too well now and they give him a pain. Live and learn.

Dwight's friend Hsai Piu has mixed himself up in this dope as quite a leader. They seem to think he is trying to make himself strong with the party and is making trouble and working up parades and all so he can get in spite of having tried to help out last year in furthering the Nationalist Party. That's the way this new outfit works. You must belong if you are a Hunanese and expect to have any sort of face in the province. Many hate to join but most of them do not dare take an active part so they will be accepted. This lad, Hsia, was off at committee meetings and all that sort of stuff when his wife "gradually" went into labor. He didn't seem to notice it for a couple of days, and by that time there was a transverse position with a presenting arm which was poor business, and which meant the loss of the child and nearly the loss of his wife. He rallied round the flag all right then, and practically "specialled" her night and day, just at the time when the nurses were being funny and ambling off duty and being more irresponsible than usual. It was a good lesson for him, but hard on the family. However, human life is not so highly valued as in the foolish western countries, so they will probably recover their spirits.

My horse got so thin and the weather so bad I gave him away to the Tyngs in the city for their kids to ride when they came back for Christmas vacation. Now it has suddenly turned bright but the kids are already home so I am temporarily stung. I just had a snappy pair of riding boots made too, which seems a bit sad. However, I shall borrow the animal back if they fatten him up properly after the kids depart again. That's one thing I shall miss when I return to the Land of the Free.

December 27, 1926 ~ Changsha

Dear Mother,

Christmas has come and gone and we are still here on the spot. I had expected so many times to be out of here by then that it seems odd to still be here. Everything is very quiet and peaceful at present and it is hard to believe we were in such a stew a few weeks ago. There were all sorts of rumors about trouble on Christmas Day, parades and demonstrations of an anti-Christian nature but there was very little of it here. I have heard there were places up country where some Mission property was destroyed and some Christians were treated roughly.

There is an impression around here that somewhere the demonstration was planned but called off at the last minute. At any rate we had a very quiet day. We entertained the unmarried at our house, 10 in number, which seems a small aggregation compared with the crowds we have had in past years. This included Miss Gage and Sunny Lewis, we other three nurses, Ota Walters, the surviving bachelor Southard Menzel, Dr. Houston's stepson John Walton, Frank Hutchins and Charlie Keller. They had all sent over their stockings and we distributed the presents and then had breakfast of waffles. Your picture and book had arrived, for which I thank you very much.

I think the photo is very good and am mighty pleased to have it, as it is the only family picture I have. I had hoped that perhaps Eunice's would come through with a contribution as they gush a way of doing so that I could show the world my handsome niece and nephews. Of course there is yet time, as we receive driblets of mail every day with occasional packages thrown in.

Besides your presents, I got a book from Elizabeth Henry, *Harmer John,* by Hugh Walpole, a towel from Aunt Hattie, and some hankies from Mrs. Shibley. There were many joke presents as usual, including a swell hankie with a picture of Sun Yat-sen in the corner. His pictures are all over everywhere these days. I also received perfume and soap, there being some very fine brands of both in the department store here, French varieties, a seal with my Chinese character on it, more hankies, a comb and a watch for duty use, also with a picture of Sun Yat-sen on it from Charlie Keller. I had taken him and Frank Hutchins shopping the day before and we had a very enjoyable time. We had been reading *Gentlemen Prefer Blondes* so I was sure they would know what I meant by admiring everything in sight. Frank gave Jess and me each a Damascene (having to do with Damascus design) bracelet, which he had bought in Japan, apropos, a remark that, "A kiss on the hand is very pleasant but a diamond bracelet lasts longer.

Frank and Charlie and I belong to a family now formed when we thought the servants were going on strike and that I would go over there and be their housekeeper. We are "Teria" family, they being "Hys" and "Wis" and I being "Caffy." We have great jokes over it as you can imagine. They both seem to have recovered very successfully from their matrimonial venture and near-venture. Jess and I went down to the Presbyterian Mission for tiffin, a ladies' party.

In the afternoon, I went riding with Southard. I have given away my horse, but I borrowed it back for the occasion, as I knew the new owners would not be coming out that day. The weather has suddenly become gorgeous and it was an ideal day for riding. I had on my new riding boots, which are very stylish and very tight around the tops. I had them made without trying them on over thick trousers I wear in the winter. Before we had ridden very far I had to get off. As a result I had to have Southard help me pull the blooming things off while I braced against my pony and he against his. A huge crowd gathered to see what it was all about, though I doubt if they ever got the straight of it. I had on my orange turtleneck sweater I knit this summer and which is startling in itself without a boot pulling to add to the excitement. We had a grand ride and ended for tea with the Heinrichsons where we saw Miss Hasie and had a chance to wish her Merry Christmas.

We flew back home and then dressed for dinner, which we had at the Rollins'. Charades were the chief entertainment, the prize being the word "Anomaly" and "An - amah-Li. It was very cleverly worked out and had us all stumped. They just kept doing crazy inconsistent things and then bringing in this dumb amah (female servant), who kept saying her name was Li. We gave "Manifold," that is "Manna-fold" which Sunny Lewis guessed out of thin air with no thought what it might be at all. We could have choked her for making so accurate a mistake.

This whole situation is not without its humorous aspects. Take the case of Dr. Walters and her amah. They have had the lady working for them since summer and she has been getting lazier and lazier all the time. Dr. Walters was good enough to pay the tuition of her two kids at school but of course she was not satisfied and like so many domestics thought that it meant she would have everything and need not do any work.

When the schools stopped, she brought the children to Ota's house to live and then asked permission after they had been there for a while. Ota decided she had had enough, and would like to fire her. According to the new labor union regulations, we are not allowed to fire servants without presenting the case to the union and getting their consent. Therefore, Ota wrote a letter explaining the amah was lazy and did not do her work properly and related the incident of the kids. The union replied she had not enough evidence. It seems the cook also wants to get rid of the amah so he suggested several small dishonesties were reported to the union.

This local branch then had a meeting and decided it would be all right to let her go with an extra month's wages. They thought it was all settled and then the old head coolie from Yali, Goliath, who is the branch head out here came along and said they had their instructions from headquarters they would not be allowed to fire her after all, and if they did it would mean they could have no women servants anymore, either regularly or by the day or for piece work, which was a neat little stunt and would cut out the charwoman who comes every day to empty slops. Isn't that a neat turn? What I would call a very telling way to get them where they can't do anything.

Our new Dean Tsao Tse Koo is not panning out very heavily, because he received a letter from the Changsha Dispensary Association saying that he is a "running dog" and a "foreign slave" and has no business trying to tell the nurses how to behave. I must say that I am inclined to agree with them there, but still his intentions are good, I believe. He has his proctor out here and he acts as a go-between the nurses and us. One office man told me today that this proctor has had considerable experience with students in different places and does not think that these kids act so badly due to their strict discipline in the past. They may think that Miss Gage doesn't know her stuff but they have to hand it to her; she gets results of law and order and decency.

During the past few days, some of the best pupils have gone home and the worst ones are all left. Some of them think they want to go too but they don't seem to have the nerve to pull out, the poor little timid dears. There have been several of them come and ask Miss Gage to please recommend them to other hospitals. Can you beat that for nerve, after the way they have talked about her? They are beginning to get a bit disgusted over things, that the school has not reopened again and there don't seem to be any teachers, but we are trying to play their own watchful waiting game, and it may fool them in the end.

As Dr. Chu says, " We must all sit down tightly." We hear all sorts of rumors about the post office. At any rate the other man has temporarily deposed the commissioner because he has not granted them raises of wage and all the other demands. The poor man has no personal responsibility in the matter. He received his instructions from Peking and yet he is the goat here. Their servants have had to go on strike and so their place has been picketed. They feel very sorry for themselves naturally and we feel sorry too.

We've just had a struggle getting the graduates moved over to live in the hospital. The pupils do not include them in their business. In fact, the graduates as hospital employees are not in the students' union. The answer to the moving is the support for the nursing school will stop the first of the year and I don't know where the money for feeding the gang will come from.

If we have the grads here then the food for the pupils can be stopped without starving our grads. That's the way it looks on paper and it sounds not so bad but they fool us somehow. They are bound to get this hospital under their control—the Kuomintang that is—and they'll get it eventually. I don't know how many strikes and rumors of strikes it will be necessary to have before the final transfer comes, but I am enough of a fatalist, or whatever you want to call it, to be absolutely certain it is coming. And, then, what for us?

First we were all afraid we'd be sent home and now we are all afraid we won't. We'll have to wait for all the holy old blokes in New Haven to decide about it.

We went over to the Island yesterday and had a party for the sailors. It is an annual affair and consists of "wrestling" with them for an afternoon in what might be called a "tea dance." It is quite strenuous but is all in a good cause and we have a good time because they do. There was the usual variety there, some very callow and some very wise and some rather hard-boiled. The gunboat Captain's wife was the host. She is a very pleasant person and has been here for about two months. When she first came they lived in Dr. Hume's house out here, but later moved to the island. They have two small youngsters who used to have a great time playing with the Hails and Harveys.

Dwight and Jo sent me a copy of Milt Gross's *Hiawatta, witt No Odder Poems* and a copy of *Dracula*. I would say they have very lurid taste. The Hiawatta is terrible, but rather amusing. He did so well in his "Nize Baby." This is a bit of an anticlimax.

I remember hearing Jerry Shibley describe reading *Dracula* when he was coming home on a ship from France after the war and having his hair stand on end, and his flesh creep. Just now, Charlie Keller and I are reading it. That is to say he is reading it out loud while I knit him a sweater. Sort of a bargain. Judging by the book size, and even considering his bulk, I think we will finish about the same time. It is a very cozy way to pass the time and we have a very pleasant evening every now and then with it. As there is no college or middle school and the hospital work is light, we have time to spend on such diversions. It is very cozy.

I keep wondering if the apples are on the way. One minute I am sorry they are coming because we may have gone, and then I am glad to think they are on the way because we are still here and would welcome them. Other people on the campus would be glad to buy them, I am sure, if they are still good by the time they reach here. The freight rates have gone up so much I'm afraid they may be expensive but they'll be worth it.

Speaking of expenses, do you think there are any sorts of curios or wearing apparel or any other kinds of Chinese goods I would be wise to invest in, and bring home for sale either this spring if I come then, or at least in the summer? I haven't very happy memories of my efforts before, but perhaps you might have heard someone express a desire for something, or you might have some brilliant inspirations. I would not be averse to making a few pennies but I am not keen on loading up with junk I couldn't dispose of or would be white elephants on my hands. I do not feel the linen is such a poor investment because I can use it eventually and would like to have what there is left saved for me to look over when I come home.

I haven't had any Changsha rugs made yet as things have been so upset it is hard to get those people to come out to foreign compounds to do anything. However, I think I shall take a chance and have some made for the family at any rate. Speaking of rugs, I tremble to think where those of Austin's may be or will be. I have heard nothing of them since September though to the best of my knowledge they are still at the Standard Oil Co. in Changchow. I have written to Les Walker asking him to get them back to Peking and then he can send them to me in Shanghai when I go through, whenever that will be. This uncertainty is rather terrible but there is nothing to be done about it so we develop a Chinese placidity and hope everything will be all right after a while. Perhaps it is just as well not to tell Austin the fate of his rugs until they are definitely lost or until they are recovered and then it will be no harm to tell how close a shave they had.

The widower of my friend, Mary Aplin Barton, who was in my class in Holyoke and died last year in Shanghai, is now in Changsha. This is a poor time of year to be introduced to this place, as the river is low, there is lots of sand and not much green. However, there has been much gaiety and the weather has been bright so he thinks it not altogether hopeless.

January 27, 1927 ~ Changsha

American Consulate Changsha, China

Strictly Confidential

Dear Miss Smith,

Recent advice has come to me from an authoritative source, which renders it imperative, I request you to withdraw immediately from Changsha to a larger port in China where protection can more readily be given. If practicable I advise you to withdraw from China.

Please avail yourself of the first opportunity to depart for Hankou.

Very respectfully yours,
J. C. Vincent
American Vice Consul in Charge.

February 4, 1927 ~ Changsha

"He says no one could handle the nursing work as well as you."

YALE IN CHINA

Office of the Treasurer

Address reply to
Dickson H. Leavens, Treasurer

CHINA ADDRESS,
Changsha, China

HOME OFFICE,
5 White Hall,
New Haven, Conn.

Telegrams
Yali, Changsha

Yamis New Haven

MISSIONS CODE

Changsha, China
Feb. 4, 1927

Miss Smith,

I had a call from Tsao Tse Koo this afternoon, who says they have had a meeting and decided to keep hospital open. He asked me to ask you if you would stay on. He says they will get rid of the men nurses. He also said he saw Branch Wednesday, and that he said he would come back in that case, but whether that is so or not, I do not know.

He asked me to find out from you whether you would stay, and let him know. He says no one could handle the nursing work as well as you.

Sincerely

EPILOGUE

After leaving China, Harriet went on to complete a stellar career as a medical professional, culminating in her retirement as the Dean of the University of Washington School of Nursing.

She developed a very strong family relationship, becoming the matriarchal center of the extended Smith/ McComb family. During and following her retirement, she continued building a friendship base worldwide and traveling extensively (Europe, Asia, Australia, the Pacific, New Zealand, etc.), yet never visited her beloved China again. Harriet, a.k.a "Hat" and "Aunt Hat," always maintained a keen interest in the world at large and sought new adventure to her last days.

Harriet at 90 Years Old

Much to her credit was her universal appeal to all ages and stations in life, she having great respect for all, being genuinely interested in all she met, King or pauper.

Twenty some years after her death, she continues to be a center of conversation among those who knew and loved her. She has taken on a near "legend" quality. For years following her death, we would discover people who had dealings with Hat, professionally, as her students, and in other roles. Once they learned of our relationship with Hat we would have hours of memories to share. Nearly everyone agrees that upon meeting Harriet, you just knew you were in the presence of a truly exceptional human.

We only wish you could have enjoyed knowing "Aunt Hat."

More of Charlie Keller

P.S. You may wonder what became of her fiancé, since her marriage to Charles Keller obviously never took place. The following letter was found, which was probably written around 1960. It provides additional insight to their relationship and Hat's adventuresome attitudes and zest for life. A woman ahead of her times in so many ways.

I did not know Chas. for very long or very well, but somehow our acquaintance has remained very vivid over the past 35 Years. Sometimes early romances take on an aura of exaggerated importance and glamor over the years, but in our case it was really not a romantic affair. We were both in our middle twenties, half way round the world from our respective homelands, he from England and I from the United States; both of us were in a city in the interior of China, but beyond that there was little similarity of background past or present.

He was a junior member of a large oil company and was assigned to the job of checking up on local Chinese representatives in the small towns up country. I was employed in an American-supported hospital engaged in nursing education and supervision.

He had been born in China and spoke one of the local dialects very well, but I had come only recently and my knowledge of the language was limited to the gradual progress I was making with a dear old Chinese tutor who fortunately knew no English at all.

Chas. was not an important person by any gauge you might use. He was not an outstanding artist, or a well-known industrialist or author. He did not excel in any sport or craft, but just happened to be a most unforgettable character.

The other young men in his mess kept referring to Chas. during my first months in China, and one day while we were having tea, he appeared. I had not been prepared for his appearance, which was one of the unforgettable aspects. He was quite short, clad in khaki-colored open-necked shirt and shorts and stockings to his bare knees. His hair, which was in need of cutting, was of the same shade as his clothes, parted on the side and with a long lock hanging over his eyes. Unlike the stereotyped picture of the typical reserved Englishman, he had a cheerful broad grin on his face, revealing a space of a missing tooth in the front. It was impossible to think of him other than as a friend from the very first meeting. A cheerful atmosphere would develop whenever he appeared.

His name of course was Charles, but he always signed it with the abbreviation, and we immediately called him "Chas" - period! To him this was a colossal joke, because "you poor benighted colonials do not seem to realize that a sentence ends with a 'full stop.' Now I ask you!" This led to other comparisons of English-American terms, leading through the garter-suspender-braces group through the cracker-biscuit-bun department to the sweater-jumper-tunic constellation, and many others. His comments were always generously interspersed with "My sainted aunt" and "my holy god-mother" and things were always qualified with "jolly old" or "poor benighted" or "dashed fine" or other phrases which most of us had always associated with P.G. Wodehouse. It had never occurred to me that there were people who actually talked that way. As a matter of fact Chas. really did not use those expressions in serious conversation, but mainly to entertain his uninitiated American friends.

When he discovered how enchanted we were with this kind of English, he could readily be persuaded to tell us good old nursery stories in that style, Goldilocks and the Three Bears and Little Red Riding Hood. "Oh, I say, some filthy blighter has been messing about with my porridge," and "Oh I say, Granny, but you do have jolly fine teeth."

I have felt exceedingly grateful to Chas. for helping me to overcome an acute discomfort I had experienced ever since my early teens when I began to grow taller than any boys my own age. This went on until as an adult I was also taller than most men I seemed to meet. Chas. was probably a good six inches shorter than I, and I am sure his lack of height had been as great a source of regret to him as my added height had been to me. But he made a cheerful joke of it, and we found that as dancing partners we were unique and entertaining to our friends. "You steer and I'll push," he would say, insisting that he could not see over my shoulder. But when we came to the Tango, we really achieved a performance for which we became famous among our associates.

A mark of a true friend is one who would give you the shirt off his back. By this standard he was truly a friend, because I acquired not one but three shirts. It happened that he had had some made of grass linen. They were beautiful shirts, but unfortunately due to a fault in the cloth or some carelessness in their laundering, had developed weak places either side of the collar in front where it showed. So the shirts were mine, and the clear area on the back was just the right size for making the kind of cap which I wore on duty.

Chas. also introduced me to a phase of life up country, which I could not otherwise have experienced. It seemed that periodically he had to take the company launch, a sort of African Queen, up one of the tributaries of the river on which our city was located, in order to inspect some of the local branches of the company. This craft was small enough to negotiate the shallow rivers, but large enough to provide an upper deck with canopy as well as a lower deck with cabin-stateroom and galley and quarters for the crew. This meant that there were sleeping accommodations for two on the upper deck, two on the lower, and crew aft. Chas. and one of his pals was to make the three-day trip over the weekend and suggested that one of my colleagues and I go along too. Obviously this was contrary to regulations, to go off like that with two men for two nights un-chaperoned, into the wilds. By this time we had been in China long enough to have discovered the fine art of dissembling, or play-acting, which meant that one could travel in disguise, and therefore one could not be recognized or questioned. This assumed that an observer would go along with the act, and usually they would, if detection would not involve them in censure or in making unpleasant decisions.

So my friend and I wandered off one Saturday morning for a "walk by the river." To be sure, we were carrying bulky bundles unlike picnic equipment, and by some curious coincidence just happened to be met at the steps leading from the end of the street into the river by the boat on which to our surprise were Chas. and his friend. In order not to appear discourteous, we accepted their invitation to step aboard, and thus we embarked on a little trip, which brought us back on Sunday evening. Imagine our surprise. We had taken the precaution of leaving word with our cook and houseboy that we were going to visit friends for a couple of days, so everything was nicely taken care of, and no one felt obliged to ask further questions.

The launch plowed slowly along, past small villages built out over the river's high water mark. We saw the familiar clothes drying on poles, the children running around clad in short shirts, heard the familiar shouts and cries, smelled the familiar odors of drying fish and human excreta. Between villages we passed little farmhouses with their dried mud bricks and thatched roofs with a clear space in front of each house where a few chickens, pigs and children were playing under the eye of an old grandmother or grandfather sitting on a chair in the shade.

The river was fairly winding and bamboo and liquid amber trees shaded it for stretches between the clear areas where rice fields drained into the river. The towpath along the bank was quite close in places, and we found we could jump off onto it where the bank was steep enough, and thus relieve the monotony of boat travel and have short exercise periods during the day. By evening we arrived at our destination and tied up at a dock along with a varied assortment of junks, motor launches, sampans and houseboats. There was a lot of activity, loading and unloading, selling all kinds of wares to the people on the boats, arguing and laughing.

Chas. instructed us to prepare for dinner ashore with the local representative as host. Having limited wardrobe, we did our best to look presentable and started off for the shop. Up to this time our only experience in eating Chinese food away from home had been in the home of Chinese or colleagues, or in some of the city restaurants. This, however, was really (foreign) the genuine unadulterated variety of local hospitality. In the first place no other women were present, in the second there were the proper total of ten people, and in the third place the service was truly Chinese. The host was not a person of high rank, but a merchant with some status in the community. This was not a meal to impress foreigners, but a special dinner for a business supervisor.

In spite of my language limitations, I clearly understood the host's issues regarding the kind of women Chas. had accompanying him . . .

APPENDIX

The Seattle Smiths and Yale-in-China ~ 1912 – 1926

During the first quarter of the twentieth century, one American family had a unique relationship to the City of Changsha, Hunan Province. Three Smiths from Seattle, Washington—a brother and sister, and their older cousin—spent a combined total of fourteen years in Changsha between 1912 and 1926, working at the Yali School and the Hunan-Yale Hospital that had been established at that city in 1908 under the auspices of Yale University. Their experiences demonstrate in a small way what can happen when persons from different cultural backgrounds—Chinese and American—reach out with energy and good will to join in a cooperative endeavor.

Harold V. Smith, 1890-1984

When Ya-Li School was established, Yale University initiated a program in which some of its new graduates would spend one or two years in Changsha, teaching at the new school. They were known as "the Yali Bachelors." Harold Smith, a member of the Class of 1912, was an early participant in the program. He spent a year (1912-13) at Yali. Inspired by his experience, Harold returned home for further education, and then went back to Yali in 1916 to teach in the Department of Geology. In the early 1920s he served briefly as Interim Treasurer of Yali. He returned to the United States in 1923.

Harriet H. Smith, 1897-1990;

Harriet was Harold's younger cousin. After graduating from Mount Holyoke College, she enrolled in the Nursing program at St. Luke's Hospital in New York City. When she graduated from that program in 1920, she returned home to Seattle. After a year-long stint as a private nurse, she decided to join her cousin in Changsha. She served as a nursing Supervisor in the Hunan-Yale Hospital from September 1921 to August 1924. She returned again to Seattle for about 18 months before being recalled to Changsha in February 1926 to become Superintendent of Nurses for one year.

Dwight C. Smith, 1900-1985

Dwight was Harriet's younger brother. As an undergraduate at Yale he determined to devote his life to China, as a missionary. Upon graduation from Yale in 1922, he became a Yali Bachelor and spent two years teaching English in Changsha. He returned to Yale in 1924 as a Divinity School student, fully intending to return to China; but during his final school year, 1926-27, China unexpectedly closed its borders to foreigners and he was unable to return.

The three cousins all were impressed by their stays at Yali, and in the years to come spoke warmly of their times in Changsha. Perhaps Harold best expressed their feelings. As he wrote later to his college classmates, that first year "completely changed my plans for the future. So now instead of looking forward to the routine-like life of an engineer in (the United States), I anticipate taking part in the absorbing and tremendously significant work being done at Yale-in-China." He added:

> "What can be more interesting than this close association with another race, especially when one is able to meet and know all classes from servants to students, scholars and officials. They seem so superficially different and yet prove to be fundamentally similar to us, that it gives one fresh ideas and a new attitude toward other people. The effect on everyone who has this experience is to make him a broader man, with wider sympathies...."

One of the great sources of satisfaction to be derived from a year at Yali is the feeling of a real share in a great constructive movement that is playing a significant role in the transformation of China. It increases a man's enthusiasm and interest when he realizes that the students with whom he comes in contact are the pick of the land and destined to be leaders in the coming generation…. The barriers of race are soon removed, and when once their friendship has been won, I have found the Chinese peculiarly human and companionable…. This close contact with another race, and the opportunity of seeing them through their own eyes, is rarely given to the casual traveler. "Yali School (http://en.wikipedia.org/wiki/Yali_School)

From Wikipedia, the free encyclopedia

History

Founded in 1906 by Yale-in-China, now known as the Yale-China Association, Yali School has been known throughout China for its quality instruction, both as an American-owned private school during the first half of the 20th century and as a public school since then. The name Yali (pinyin: Yǎ Lǐ) comes from the Analects of Confucius, meaning elegance of expression (ya) and propriety of conduct (li), and is a transliteration of Yale in early-20th century. Yali's school colors are blue, white (Yale colors) and red (China), as appear on the school uniform.

Founding Years

Brownell Gage, Warren Seabury, Lawrence Thurston, and Arthur Williams, all graduates of Yale College in the 1890s, founded Yale-in-China, and brought the mission to Changsha between the years of 1901 and 1905. In 1906, the mission's preparatory school, or the Yali School, began operations. During the same year, Edward H. Hume, M.D., commenced the medical work in Changsha. His experiences are described in his 1946 book *Doctors East, Doctors West: An American Physician's Life in China*, (W. W. Norton & Company, Inc.). In 1912 Yali's first graduates received degrees.

Continued Success

The campus was dramatically expanded in 1914, and Yali became the most well-known and highly regarded education institution in the Republic of China era. By 1928, Yali started opening up its administrative and leadership roles to Chinese educators. While Yali students were known for their academic performance, they were also well-trained athletes, with the school's many athletic teams—soccer, volleyball, and track, for example—winning provincial and national tournaments.

World War II Years

In 1938, Yali students and faculty were forced to move to Yuanling in western Hunan to avoid bombing in Changsha during the Japanese invasion of China. Teaching continued in Yuanling for seven years before the School returned to Changsha in 1946.

Early PRC Years

In November 1948, the US government started evacuating Americans in China. Dr. Dwight Rugh became the last Yale-China representative in China. In 1951, Dr. Rugh was brought to the new gym on the Yali campus in a school-wide meeting to condemn "American Capitalist Invaders"; he returned to America via Hong Kong soon after. During the same year, the municipal government of Changsha took over the administration of the Yali School and changed its name to Changsha Number Five Middle School to be integrated into the city's public school system. The School's tie with Yale-China was cut off. During the next few decades, Yali experienced political turbulences that swept much of China.

Dwight Rugh is the father of Betty Jean Rugh (now BJ Elder), who grew up in Changsha and later moved to the United States with her parents. BJ Elder published a book in 2003 titled *The Oriole's Song - An American Girlhood in Wartime China* (see cited sources below), describing her childhood in Changsha on the Yali campus and the various trips she made back to China in the decades following the family's forced departure.

After the Cultural Revolution

In 1980, Yali, known at the time still as Changsha Number Five Middle School, returned to operations from a whole decade of chaos. With the new "reform and opening-up" policy instituted by Deng Xiaoping, more freedom to connect with the outside world was realized. Yali alumni from the first half of the 20th Century started working tirelessly between Changsha and New Haven, seeking to re-establish the Yale-China connection. In 1985, the School revived its relationship with the Yale-China Association and was once again known as Yali. The next year, Yale-China bachelors, now known as English Language Instructors ("ELI", also a nickname for Yalies), arrived on campus and resumed teaching responsibilities in the English Department.

Today

Since 1986, Yali has reinvented itself again as a leading secondary education institution in China. While following a standard curriculum prescribed by the Ministry of Education, it expanded its education philosophy to include extracurricular and specialty education to offer students opportunities to engage themselves in campus life in and outside the classroom. The School has received numerous provincial and national recognitions for its excellence in providing high quality education to young minds. In 1992, it became formally recognized as one of the first Provincial Key Schools in Changsha, establishing it as a premier institution in China's public school system.

At the same time, with its long history of international engagement, Yali has reached out to institutions in many other countries and established sister school relationships internationally. In 2001, the School received a delegation from Yale University led by Yale's president, Richard Levin, in celebration of both the Centennial of the Yale-China Association as well as the Tercentennial of Yale University. In 2006, Yali celebrated its own Centennial, bringing back alumni/ae and former teachers from all parts of the world.

Note from the Authors

The more we worked with Harriet's letters, the more appreciation we gained about "Aunt Hat," her life and times; and, what a rich story she had to share with the family and the world.

We can only hope we have captured more than just the basics, but the real essence of Harriet: Her brilliance, humanity, adventure, and humor.

The good news: We have four more years (1921 – 1924) of letters to share with you.

Carolyn and Dennis